# The media's watchin
# Here's a sampling of

"For those hoping to climb the ladder of success, [Vault's] insights are priceless."
– *Money magazine*

"The best place on the web to prepare for a job search."
– *Fortune*

"[Vault guides] make for excellent starting points for job hunters and should be purchased by academic libraries for their career sections [and] university career centers."
– *Library Journal*

"The granddaddy of worker sites."
– *US News and World Report*

"A killer app."
– *New York Times*

One of Forbes' 33 "Favorite Sites"
– *Forbes*

"To get the unvarnished scoop, check out Vault."
– *Smart Money Magazine*

"Vault has a wealth of information about major employers and job-searching strategies as well as comments from workers about their experiences at specific companies."
– *The Washington Post*

"A key reference for those who want to know what it takes to get hired by a law firm and what to expect once they get there."
– *New York Law Journal*

"Vault [provides] the skinny on working conditions at all kinds of companies from current and former employees."
– *USA Today*

# Decrease your T/NJ Ratio
## (Time to New Job)

Use the Internet's most targeted job search tools for finance professionals.

## Vault Finance Job Board

The most comprehensive and convenient job board for finance professionals. Target your search by area of finance, function, and experience level, and find the job openings that you want. No surfing required.

## VaultMatch Resume Database

Vault takes match-making to the next level: post your resume and customize your search by area of finance, experience and more. We'll match job listings with your interests and criteria and e-mail them directly to your inbox.

# VAULT CAREER GUIDE TO SALES & TRADING

# VAULT CAREER GUIDE TO SALES & TRADING

**GABRIEL KIM**
**AND THE STAFF OF VAULT**

Library of Congress CIP Data is available.

ISBN 1-58131-252-0

Printed in the United States of America

# ACKNOWLEDGEMENTS

**Gabriel Kim's acknowledgements:**

To Irene, my best friend and love for life.
Special thanks also to our dear parents in Winnipeg and New York.

**Vault's acknowledgements:**

Vault would like to acknowledge the assistance and support of Matt Doull, Ahmad Al-Khaled, Lee Black, Eric Ober, Hollinger Ventures, Tekbanc, New York City Investment Fund, American Lawyer Media, Globix, Hoover's, Glenn Fischer, Mark Fernandez, Ravi Mhatre, Carter Weiss, Ken Cron, Ed Somekh, Isidore Mayrock, Zahi Khouri, Sana Sabbagh and other Vault investors. Many thanks to our loving families and friends.

# Table of Contents

# Introduction

If you believe in the efficient markets hypothesis, then you should not be considering a career in sales and trading. An old joke about the hypothesis goes something like this:

> A finance professor and a student are walking down a busy sidewalk. Along the way, the professor discusses the efficient markets hypothesis with his student, who is staring down in studious thought. The student catches a glimpse of a $20 bill on the sidewalk, and he stops to pick it up. After pocketing the bill, the student runs to catch up with the professor. The excited student asks the professor if he had seen the bill. The professor, without skipping a beat, quips, "My dear student, have you not been listening to any part of the efficient markets that I've been talking about? Yes, I saw the $20, but I knew that my eyes must have been deceiving me. Efficient markets theory dictates that it couldn't possibly have been there, since someone else would have already picked it up."

If you're considering a career in sales and trading, you probably don't believe in the efficient markets hypothesis, or at least don't believe that markets are perfectly efficient – and are willing to wager your career on it.

Wall Street is an exciting place to be, and sales and trading (the "sell-side" of the Street), is one of the most exciting areas. It's an extremely competitive business – at times it's downright ruthless. If you're a market junkie and bought your first stock when you were in third grade, then trading is definitely the place for you. If prior to considering a career change to S&T, you made a career selling ice to the Eskimos, then instiutional or private client sales on Wall Street might be the right place for you. And even if you were a security guard or a consultant, or studied arts or sciences in school, sales and trading might still be for you.

The pace of sales and trading is fast and furious in the heat of battle, but passion and initiative can produce extraordinary results. Whether you're just exploring sales and trading as a potential career option, or you're someone who's wanted to trade stock since the third grade, this Vault guide can help you prepare for that job interview, nail it and hit the ground running when you start. Good luck!

# THE SCOOP

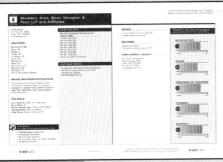

# Sales and Trading Basics

## CHAPTER 1

## What is Sales and Trading?

If you've ever been to an investment banking trading floor, you've witnessed the pandemonium. Before the market opens, the trading desk seems like a reasonable place to work. Traders are monitoring flickering screens, and salesmen are having seemingly pleasant telephone conversations. But once the market opens, there's an eruption of activity – the salesmen and traders are yelling, swearing and shouting at each other. The exchange floor is even more chaotic. Tempers are short, nerves are frayed, and there are bits of confetti flying around everywhere. If the market is tanking or diving, the sound and fury of trading activity rises palpably. What's most impressive about all of this is that beneath this buzz of unruly activity on the desk or the floor, traders are making prices, salesmen are shopping merchandise and millions of shares of stock are being transacted every time someone says "done."

### I saw the movie "Wall Street." Is sales and trading like that?

*Wall Street* is a movie worth watching because it gives you a very good idea of what it takes to get in the door (unbridled ambition) and what it takes to stay there (the ability to generate profits). In some circles it's considered required viewing for any professional entering the business. In the movie, Bud Fox is a rookie broker who "bags the elephant" (lands a huge client), Gordon Gekko. Gordon Gekko decides to give Fox a chance, after he agrees to help Gekko trade on inside information and Fox starts to generate big commissions trading Gekko's orders. This much of the story is plausible. Then, the movie takes a somewhat unrealistic turn as Fox's character transforms from a broker into a nascent corporate takeover artist. Fox helps Gekko take over his father's airline, Blue Star Airlines. In the process, Gekko stabs Bud in the back by trying to break up the airline. The story is compelling, but if you get a start in private client services like Fox (nobody is called a broker anymore), don't expect to be pitching mergers and acquisition deals to your clients. This is the responsibility of the firm's investment bankers. On the other hand, Bud's never-ending quest to "bag the elephant" is something you can expect to relate to if you get your start as a salesperson on Wall Street.

## I saw the movie "Boiler Room." Is sales and trading like that?

Hopefully not. *Boiler Room* describes the exploits of a pump-and-dump operation. Pump-and-dump is the practice of buying low-priced shares of (usually) illegitimate companies. Salespeople then go out and apply high-pressure sales tactics to unload this worthless stock on retired folks in Florida and farmers in Iowa. As the share price begins to rise, the unscrupulous broker then dumps the shares that he bought at substantially lower prices on unsuspecting buyers. This activity is completly illegal, even for Ben Affleck and Vin Diesel. If you find yourself working in this type of environment, get out, unless you look good in stripes.

There are several aspects of this movie worth noting, however. First, every self-respecting salesperson and trader has the lines to *Boiler Room* memorized. Second, the movie accurately portrays a pervasive culture of greed underlying this entire business. People join this business for no other reason than money, so don't expect to be able to tell your friends that you're providing an invaluable service to society by selling municipal bonds or trading exotic options. Finally, as depicted in the movie, Wall Street trading desks remain a male-dominated macho work environment. We'll explore diversity issues with respect to women in S&T later on this guide.

## So what is sales and trading?

At this point, we know that sales and trading isn't exactly what we see on the movies. So what is sales and trading? Salespeople work with customers on what is called "the buy-side," selling them large amounts of securities like stocks, bonds or currencies. The largest customers on the buy-side are typically institutions (such as mutual funds or pension funds) that manage assets for others. Salespeople who sell to these institutions are identified by a variety of titles: institutional salesperson, sales-trader or research salesperson. Salespeople who sell to smaller institutions or wealthy individuals are called private client services (PCS) professionals.

Traders watch the market and trade orders for customers. The trader never talks directly to the customer; it's the job of the salesperson (institutional or

PCS) to act as intermediary. The trader uses an array of computer systems to track the market and to execute orders.

## What is the buy-side?

The buy-side refers to the investment management firms, pension funds and trusts that buy stocks, bonds and other securities from the "sell-side."

## What is the sell-side?

The sell-side refers to Wall Street investment banks that sell stocks, bonds and other securities to the buy-side. The numerous sales and trading programs that recruit on-campus are for the sell-side firms.

# S&T and Investment Banking

## How is sales and trading different from investment banking?

There are several ways to compare and contrast the differences between investment banking and sales and trading. The first is the actual work that they do and the time in which this work is done. Investment bankers primarily help to raise money for clients through stock or bond offerings or advise clients on mergers or acquisitions. The endless flow of pitchbooks (PowerPoint presentations to clients), the detailed financial modeling and around-the-clock client schmoozing are all focused on achieving one result: a deal that will generate substantial fee income for the investment bank. This fee is calculated as a percentage of the deal (for example, a percentage of the money raised by an initial public offering). Investment bankers work for months – even years – to generate one deal, schmoozing comany execs until the company is ready to raise money or acquire a company. But when the company is ready and hires the bank to chip them, the reward for the bank is substantial.

Salespeople and traders also work on deals – every trade is a deal – and also entertain clients. Compared to investment banking, however, it takes much less time to consummate a transaction in S&T. Typical trades are consummated in seconds or minutes, and the average fee per trade is measured in cents per share traded rather than as a percentage of the deal's proceeds.

Another big difference between S&T and I-banking is the lifestyle. Sales and trading professionals are the first-in-and-first-out in the investment bank. To get a jumpstart on the trading day, salespeople and traders normally take the earliest train into work. But they are the first ones out of the office, leaving shortly after the markets close. Salespeople and traders also never work weekends – trading desks are completely abandoned on the weekends. In contrast, investment bankers are expected to be their desks during the weekdays and weekends, at all hours and throughout major holidays. If you ever want to see a sad sight, go to one of the major investment banks on Christmas Day or Easter. Around lunch time, you'll see investment banking analysts trickle down from their cramped bullpens to pick up their food orders from the delivery guy. Sales and trading is a sprint; investment banking is an endless marathon that rarely ever stops for anything.

## Why do investment banks have sales and trading departments?

The most important function of a sales and trading department at an investment bank is, of course, to make money. An investment bank collects significant fees every time its sales and trading professionals execute a deal for clients. Traders and salespeople add incrementally to the bottom line through daily profit and loss and commissions, and raise the profile of the firm in the marketplace.

But there are ancillary benefits to having a strong S&T department. Investment banks provide capital raising and mergers and acquisition advisory services. Salespeople and traders are needed to create and maintain an active secondary market in these new issues. (Investments that are simply bought and held, such as life insurance, do not have secondary markets. Secondary markets exist to allow investors to buy and sell investments such as stock even after an initial public offering.) Most large investment banks target their secondary market activities towards issues that will support the primary market activities and capital raising efforts of the investment bank (for example, a client company's IPO). Companies and other entities that raise money by issuing stock or bonds are primarily concerned with how much money they can raise and at what price, but they're also concerned with the ability of the investment bank to properly distribute shares of the new issue and the ability of the investment bank and its syndicate (other investment banks partnering in the deal) to actively trade the new issue. An investment bank's market share of the daily trading volume in the issuer's stock can often be a decisive factor in deciding which bank gets to bring the new issue to market. Of course, to do this properly, traders will also trade stocks that are important in the context of the overall marketplace.

# Sales and Trading Culture

### The sales and trading team environment

Sales and trading is a symbiotic relationship. Salespeople need traders and traders need salespeople. Salespeople wouldn't be able to provide liquidity to customers without traders, and traders would be twiddling their thumbs all day long without customer orders to trade. This simple reality is sometimes lost during the course of the trading day, when traders routinely rip into salespeople, and salespeople shake their heads as they pick up the phone to give reports to their customers.

Let's take a closer look at why salespeople and traders often find themselves at odds. Let's say a trader just bought 500,000 shares of Precision Orthopedic Supplies (POS) from Fluke Investment Bank and makes a big spectacle about the trade, yelling at a salesperson something like, "That's not the right price, Dave, but you know that's what Fluke always does. These guys are trying to sandbag me again." Here, the trader is concerned that he has bought the stock at too high a price, albeit from an important customer. The salesperson may shoot back something like, "Come on, you know Joe over at Fluke. You had dinner with him last week! Play nice... you know this order grows." Here, the salesperson is telling the trader that doing the trade to keep the relationship with Fluke strong will pay off in the long run.

The trader is basically trying to protect himself from the wrath of his boss in the event that POS shares plummet immediately after he buys the shares from Fluke. The salesperson is trying to protect himself from the wrath of the boss by mentioning what a great account Fluke is and how important this account is to the success of the desk. If only one side says something, and the share price of POS goes on to hit the fan, the boss will harass the other side for a full accounting of his reckless actions: "Capital doesn't grow on trees. What kind of a stupid decision happened here?!" However, if both sides yell at each other, then at least it becomes a little harder for the boss to blame either. More often than not, at the end of a profitable trading day, you'll observe the salesperson and the trader have a discreet conversation during which they basically kiss and make up. The salesperson affirms the trader's superior price-making ability, and the trader affirms the salesperson's incredibly deep and invaluable customer relationships. It's a lovefest as long as everyone's making money. The main point here is that a trading desk is a lot like a circus. Experienced salespeople and traders recognize that a lot of what goes on is for show.

At the core of why salespeople and traders routinely find themselves at odds is that traders and salespeople have different measures of performance. Traders make money by buying low and selling high. For an investor in POS, this might mean buying at $20/share and six months later, selling at $26/share. For an institutional trader, whose time horizon is measured in seconds, this means buying at $20 and selling at $20.06/share. If the trader can make 6 cents on every share traded on a million share trade, he's making 6 million pennies, or $60,000. In contrast, the salesperson is compensated by commissions (called sales credits) on each transaction. Commissions are generated entirely through volume, so the typical salesperson values size of customer trade, rather than profitability of customer trade.

Of course, in the ideal situation, traders and salespeople work together to trade the maximum amount of volume for the most profit for the firm. But at times, salespeople and traders are at odds – the vast majority of arguments that erupt throughout the trading day relate to whether you're motivated by spread or by sales credits. If salespeople and traders are not working well together, suspicion and mistrust can poison the symbiotic relationship between trader and salesperson. For example, a trader may find that he is continually "getting jammed" by a client, meaning the client (through the salesperson) has sold or bought stock to the trader at what turns out to be a bad price (this may happen, if, for example, the client happens to know something about soon-to-be released news about the company). Or, a salesperson may find that a trader is only offering poor prices or poor volumes to the client, even though the stock may be moving at large volumes or at better prices through other firms. The salesperson is stuck with giving "pathetic reports" about what the trader is willing to buy or sell to his client, even though the client can see that other firms are willing to do better (in terms of either price or volume).

## The colorful personalities

Look through any sell-side firm's recruiting literature and you'll quickly learn what qualities are valued in salespeople and traders. Salespeople prize the ability to schmooze with clients, which requires superior communication skills, outgoing personalities and a sharp wit. Traders tend to be more cerebral, more analytical and they generally consider themselves to be smarter than salespeople. Traders need to be good at handling stressful situations and exuding a sense of calm and control even when situations are quickly spiraling out of control. The interesting thing about traders and salespeople is that there's a strong stereotype for how they should act and what qualities they should demonstrate, so part of the learning curve in any sales and trading environment is developing the right mannerisms and quirks that reflect the desirable qualities.

Effective salespeople and traders are good communicators. This applies not just with respect to clients, but also with respect to bosses. Experienced traders have an intuitive feel for murky situations, but the junior trader that is trading a pad of stocks as a substitute trader sometimes does not realize the level of communication that is demanded of them. If you have the good fortune of trading a pad early on in your career, make sure you continually communicate with your boss. The worst thing that can happen in your trading debut is that you buy 25,000 shares of XYZ stock and lose $100,000 on the position without ever talking with the boss. You've got a big fat loss for everyone to see, and guess what? Next time there's a trading seat that needs to be filled, you won't get the call. At the time, you may have thought that communicating too frequently with the boss would lead him to believe that you don't have much confidence or trading ability. Of course with a big fat loss at the end of the day, there's absolutely no doubt about it now. You can prevent this sad situation by keeping the boss updated on your trading decisions. This is difficult to do, because the natural instinct is to clam up when you're losing money. But by involving the boss, you'll get a feel for how an experienced professional looks at risk vis-à-vis a particular client, and if you're lucky, maybe the boss will even get involved in the situation.

## The people in your neighborhood

Trading desks are very impressive sights. There are rows and rows of computer monitors and hundreds of people intermittently pounding the table, yelling or staring intently at their screens. Each trading desk is organized a little differently, but there are several desk layout themes that are consistent. What you'll usually see is traders sitting separately from the salespeople. Salespeople may be situated in the middle of the desk or in the front on a slightly elevated platform. Salespeople need to be able to reach out and touch someone, so they will tend to occupy center stage. The traders surround the salespeople, and there's a little jockeying that goes on among them for who gets the good seats. A lot can be inferred from position with respect to the salespeople. The closer a trader sits to the salespeople, the more senior the trader is, or the more important that sector is for the overall desk, or both. The outskirts of the trading desk tend to be occupied by more junior traders, or by traders who are trading sectors that require less attention.

Trading desks are normally organized by sector (e.g., government bonds, high-yield bonds, etc.). Surrounding each trader, you may find one or more trading assistants/junior traders who help the senior trader trade his "pad" of stocks or bonds. Some desks feature characteristic elements. For example, if you're ever looking for a government bond desk, just look for the stars and stripes of the American flag.

# The Traders

## CHAPTER 2

## Bid and Ask Prices

**Below is a typical stock quote for IBM.**

| Bid | 80.22 | Ask | 80.23 | Last | 80.22 |
|-----|-------|-----|-------|------|-------|
| Open | 80.62 | Close | 80.47 | Change | -0.25 |
| High | 80.70 | Low | 78.47 | % Change | -0.31 |
| Volume | 5830900 | Last Size | 400 | B/A Size | 300x2000 |

This is a summary of the information traders use to transact deals for their clients. Let's take a closer look.

The bid price is 80.22 and the ask price is 80.23. You may wonder why there are two prices. This is because stocks, bonds and derivatives are negotiated markets. Think of a flea market where the vendor is trying to sell his rip-off Coach leather bags. You ask the vendor how much, and he replies $30. This is his offer or "ask price."

Getting back to IBM, the bid price is always lower than the ask price. Why is this? This is because dealers must make two-way markets in stocks. Whereas the Coach rip-off vendor is only in the business of selling fake bags at the flea market, the specialist or trader must be prepared to both buy and sell shares of IBM. The price that the dealer (trader) is willing to buy shares of IBM (in this case $80.22) is his bid price, which is always lower than his ask price. Confusion typically arises when a person looks at this quote and says, "I'd like to buy IBM for $80.22 and not a penny more." The problem with this is that the quote you're looking at is from the dealer's perspective. The price that the dealer is willing to buy at ($80.22 in this example) is your selling price (the dealer's "bid price") and the price that he's willing to sell ($80.23) is the price that you're buying (the dealer's "ask price").

The difference between the bid and ask price is called the spread. In theory, this spread is what the dealer should earn on every transaction – buying at $80.22 and selling at $80.23 all day long. If the dealer does this with 10 million shares, he'll make 10 million pennies, which adds up to a whole lot of coin ($100,000). In practice, this rarely happens, since markets fluctuate widely, and when one person wants to sell, it's normal for everyone to follow the crowd for the exits. This is why you'll often hear market makers and specialists grouse about not being able to feed their children when spreads narrow.

The "last trade" in the chart represents the last price that shares were transacted at, and the "last size" is the size of that trade, in this case 400 shares. The "B/A size" (the Bid/Ask size) indicates the size of the market. This quote indicates that the bid price is good for a trade up to 300 shares and that the ask price is good for a trade up to 2000 shares. The cumulative daily volume is indicated as 5,830,900 shares. Frequently, trade sizes and daily volumes are reported in thousands, so a 1000 share trade appears as 1 and a 100,000 share trade appears as 100.

The last aspect of the quote is the daily high and low price. On this particular day, IBM traded as high as $80.70 and as low as $78.47. Customers frequently check their executed trade price with these daily ranges to get an idea of how well they did at timing their purchase or sale. Just remember that as a trader on Wall Street you probably won't be the guy buying the stock at $78.47 or selling the stock at $80.70. These prices frequently reflect a dealer accommodating a panicked seller or an exuberant buyer.

# Providing Liquidity

At the core of what traders provide to clients is liquidity. Providing liquidity means accepting an appropriate price for a specified order quantity. This is very different from buying and selling a stock in your personal account. Typically, as a small investor, liquidity considerations are taken for granted since buying or selling 100 shares doesn't affect the price of the stock.

Institutional customers like mutual funds or pension funds, however, are always concerned about liquidity. Institutional investors own large amounts of stock or bonds, and when they want to sell, they need to sell in size. If you've ever looked at a real-time stock quote, you'll see that there are several numbers:

INTC  16.10 – 16.12   10x93

This is a quote for Intel. The 16.10 price is the price that dealers are willing to buy from customers. As discussed in the preceding section, this is called a "bid." The 16.12 price is the price that dealers are willing to sell to customers and is called an offer or "ask price." The 10 and 93 represent the size of the bid and offer in hundreds – this means that the bid is good for 1,000 shares and the offer is good for 9,300 shares. When you as a trader sell stock from this quote, you are "hitting the bid"; when you buy stock from this quote, you are "taking the offer." Often you will hear traders speak of "hitting," "whacking," "smashing," or "crushing" a stock. A good way to remember what this means is that all of the terms that describe striking a stock bring the stock price down, because you are selling the stock. A more detailed explanation of some of this lingo can be found in the sidebar "Trader Talk" found later in this chapter.

Typically, these bid and offer quantities are market aggregates – all the dealers on the street are willing to pay 16.10 for 1000 shares, after which time the bid is exhausted and the bid will adjust to a lower price as reflected in the order book on the NYSE or to a lower price on the montage for a NASDAQ security. The mechanics of bond pricing are substantively similar.

## A case study

To examine these mechanics in detail, let's look at a hypothetical situation where the mutual fund company Lucky Horseshoe Investments decides that it wants to sell 1 million shares of Intel. Let's say you are a trader working with Lucky Horseshoe. It's your job to provide liquidity in the marketplace. This means making the right price for 1 million shares. You'll have to make this decision in minutes and you'll have a salesperson ringing you every 30 seconds for updates. In this example, we'll use a lot of trading lingo explained in detail later in this chapter.

We start here:

INTC 16.10 – 16.12 10x93

Intel is an active stock, and the 16.10 bid is constantly in flux. Often, by the time the salesperson takes the order and relays the order to the trader, the market has moved:

INTC 16.07 – 16.10 23x99

You're not very happy with this situation. The stock is now offered where it was previously bid, and it appears that there's another seller trying to make a sale as well. As a trader, you're probably on the phone with the salesperson at your firm working with Lucky Horseshoe, letting the salesperson know the price is lower. The game that's being played here is that the salesperson is trying to get you to make a bid that doesn't embarrass the firm, and you are trying to protect your P&L. You'll typically give some options for the salesperson to discuss with Lucky Horseshoe Investments.

**Trader (you) :** "I'll buy 100,000 shares at 16.10 just because it was bid there when he came in and then we're working the rest of the order. [We'll discuss working orders later in the chapter.] Or else I'll buy 250,000 shares right here at 16.07 to work. I'd buy 500,000 shares at 16.00."

**Salesperson:** "Are you serious? This is Intel. We need to be size in Intel and this is Lucky Horseshoe Investments! How about 250,000 shares at 16.10, 500,000 shares at 16.07 and make a bid on the whole piece at 16.00."

**Trader:** "I don't know about that. Lucky Horseshoe really killed me last time – I lost over $50,000 and they never came back. If you need a bid on the whole piece I'll need to talk it over with the boss, but I think you're being way too aggressive. If Lucky Horseshoe leaves me a working order, then I'll do the 250,000 shares at 16.10. 50,000 more shares just came offered at a dime. [Note that the salesperson and trader are beginning to discuss prices just in terms of cents after $16.] Make the call quickly, treat the bid subject."

INTC: 16.06 – 16.10  23x599

**Salesperson:** "I'll be right back."

**Lucky Horseshoe Investments:** "What have we done?"

**Salesperson:** "I can do 250,000 shares at a dime if you leave a working order. The bid is down and there's 50,000 shares offered outside of us. Trader's still sucking wind from last time."

**Trader to salesperson:** "SHARES ARE TRADING ON THE BID!!!"

**Salesperson to Lucky Horseshoe Investments:** "Shares are trading at 6 cents."

**Trader to salesperson:** "WHAT ARE WE DOING?"

**Lucky Horseshoe Investments:** "Okay, I'll sell you 250,000 shares at 9 cents, working 750,000 shares and there's more behind it."

**Salesperson to Lucky Horseshoe Investments:** "That's done. We bought 250,000 shares at 9 cents working 750,000 shares for now. Thanks."

**Salesperson to trader:** "250,000 shares in at 9 cents, working 750,000 shares and the order grows."

**Trader:** "Great job, I appreciate that. We're working the order. Call him back and tell him I'll buy another 100,000 shares at 6 cents to keep up with the volume."

These are the conversations that you'll hear on a trading desk, and each conversation is a negotiation that requires timely communication and teamwork.

## Working orders

The most effective way to build trust in a customer-trader relationship is to get a "working order," which is simply an order that the trader can work over the course of the trading day. In setting up a working order, traders put up firm capital to get the order in the door. Once that first piece of stock is purchased, the trader will try to recover his loss and make a profit with the rest of the order. The more the working orders, the better the firm is in the long run. Good customers leave working orders, bad customers don't – everyone knows who the good and bad customers are and prices securities to them accordingly.

Getting the customer to leave a "working order" is the top priority of every salesperson. Salespeople with customers who only want to sell 100,000 shares when the bid is fading fast won't have very long careers. The salesperson acts as the intermediary between the trader and the customer – he passes along information, but more importantly, helps frame the decision making process for the customer. The salesperson is also responsible for managing the relationship with the trader – if a trader always loses money on his orders, the trader's going to make it more expensive for his customers to trade through him.

In our previous example, Lucky Horseshoe Investments turned out to be a good customer. He could have jammed the trader with stock at 10 cents, but instead offered to sell at 9 cents. In this situation, a customer without a strong working relationship with the sell-side firm might have come back and said that 250,000 shares is a disgrace, and that he should have called Morgan Stanley instead.

Note that at no time during the execution of the trade is the trader concerned with whether or not INTC is a good investment. A lot of people have the misperception that trading on Wall Street is about looking into a crystal ball and trying to divine the future of an investment. It's not – the trader's role is to provide liquidity and to determine an appropriate price given the interests of the customer and the firm. The trader knows the stock is going down and that there are other sellers in the marketplace, but his job is to accommodate the customer, take a hit on the first piece of business and hopefully work the order to the firm's advantage. The best way to think of trading is that the trader maintains an inventory and that he's trying to constantly unload this inventory into the marketplace. Ideally, at the end of the day he's completely flat (i.e., has worked out of all the positions) and has some profit to show for his efforts.

If you're a more cerebral type and enjoy performing extensive analysis before making an investment decision, then there are less flow-oriented products that you can consider, like fixed income derivatives and credit default swaps. These desks tend to do a lot of modeling before pulling the trigger on any given trade, but the role is still very clearly defined by the customer ("client-driven" rather than "proprietary"). If you enjoy working in a high intensity work environment, enjoy negotiating and have an ability to think quickly on your feet, then trading is definitely for you. If you prefer to make investments, then you should perhaps consider the investment management industry. (See the *Vault Career Guide to Investment Management* to learn more.)

## Q&A with a Junior Trader at a Bulge Bracket Firm in New York

**Q: What is your morning routine?**
My day begins at 6:30 a.m. I get in before my trader gets in to go over yesterday's trades to make sure that everything that was done yesterday matches with the trade details that are generated by our back office. The next thing I do is go over news headlines for each of our stocks. When my trader gets in around 7, I must have all of our starting positions confirmed, and somewhat more interesting, I discuss any news in our stocks to get an early idea of what my trader is thinking and to plot strategy for the day. This exercise is particularly important during earnings season, and although we try and stay as flat as possible

overnight, the reality is that this is a customer-driven business, and we frequently carry substantial positions.

Although the market opens at 9:30 a.m., it is always trading on Instinet and other electronic crossing networks. We relay any noteworthy trades or indications to our salesforce, and also review yesterday's AUTEX trade volumes. AUTEX is a self-reported trade volume advertisement that each broker-dealer updates throughout the day.

We have an internal research system that carries all the written notes that our firm's research analysts have written overnight. Of course I start with the notes that mention the stocks in my sector, but I'm a real market enthusiast and I try and read everything. It's great to be trading an industry-focused group of stocks, but it's also important to stay current with the bigger stock market picture. One of the major responsibilities I have had has been to build relationships with our firm's research analysts and to communicate timely market information from them to my trader, and also to the salesforce.

A fixture of our morning routine is the morning meeting, which is different from the morning research call. The morning meeting is an opportunity for the entire sales and trading department to get together and exchange information about large trading situations and any relevant news that may have been released overnight relating to the desk's positions. It's also a chance for us to grind the axe, so to speak. We try and anticipate what will happen throughout the trading day, especially if we had a large situation that we or our competitors are working on. We're also working closely with the sales desk to determine what is the best way to get customers to trade with us, and how to make sure that this incremental business is profitable.

Economic statistics are normally released at 8:30 a.m. I maintain an economic calendar since these numbers are frequently market-moving statistics. The market tends to focus on several economic figures at a given point in time. For example, when the economy is strong, everyone is worried about inflation, so the CPI and PPI are very closely watched. In recent years, with the economy has been weak, we've been very focused on initial jobless claims and the monthly employment report. The bond market normally reacts first, then the S&P futures react and often there are big head fakes, especially if there are large revisions in previously reported statistics.

Following the economic reports and some breakfast (which I fetch from the firm's cafeteria), my trader and I work on our indications. Indications are basically advertisements that we post to the buy-side to solicit interest in our stocks. These indications (buy or sell) are based on our prior day's customer activity, and our proprietary view on the stock. Our proprietary view is based on a combination of fundamental and technical factors. In theory, the way – indications are supposed to work is that we go out as a large buyer of say, Intel. A buy-side customer who wants to sell Intel notices our buy indication, and the trade volumes that we've been advertising. It's very possible that he then gives us a call and we negotiate a bid for some portion of the stock that we think he has for sale, and this generates an order that we are able to work throughout the day. Of course, most of the time these indications don't go nearly as well as expected. (Quotes are essentially advertising, and a trader might find that when it comes to actually hitting a bid or taking an offer, the other side may not honor the price, or may not want to leave a working order.)

The next thing we do is adjust our markets to reflect our opening indications. Other dealers are jostling in the box for position. Buyers (or dealers who want to project the image that they are buyers) are joining the bid or moving the bid up. Sellers move to the offering side, and if they have an interest in lowering the opening price (or projecting the appearance that they are sellers) will lower the offer. It's OK for markets to be locked (bid price equals offer price) or crossed markets (offer price is lower than the bid price), before the opening, but by 9:30 a.m., markets need to be unlocked and uncrossed.

**Q: What happens when the market opens?**
The first five minutes of trading are pretty crazy. The buzz that has been building in the trading room since 9:00 a.m. explodes with the opening bell, and the trader focuses on the larger situations, and pretty much leaves the rest of his pad on autopilot. My job is to make sure that we're not giving away the shop on these smaller situations. I've earned substantial trading responsibility, and my trader doesn't feel the need to micromanage every single situation. I take orders, work the orders and in the process, I am building up my relationship with the salesforce here in New York and in the regional offices. Traders need to command the respect of the salesforce, and it's been really important for me to make prices and to work with the salesforce to meet the needs of the clients. The more trades I do, the more respect I'm able to earn from my trader, from the salesforce and ultimately from our customer base.

**Q: How do you learn the business?**
I'm also always keeping involved in the situation that my trader is working on, and keeping abreast of the larger situations on the desk. I

can actually scan each trader's profit and loss on the screen, so generally looking at who's making or losing the most money is a good place to start. Learning in this business is pretty much all experiential, so the more I learn from others in terms of what works well in what situation with which individuals makes me a better trader. I need to pay special attention to the cast of characters involved – what works well for one customer doesn't always work well for another customer, and it's important to keep learning from my own mistakes as well as the mistakes of others.

But make no mistake about it, a trading desk is all about business, and you can really do yourself a big disservice by asking stupid questions at the wrong time. Keep a notebook, write down your questions and at the end of the day after the market is closed, try and work these questions into your conversation with the trader. There's a smart way to ask questions and a stupid way to ask questions, so be smart about learning. Having said that, there's a grace period for every new hire, so the time to ask stupid questions (i.e., "How do I read this quote?") is at the beginning of your tenure.

**Q: What makes a good trader?**

Well, we've already touched on a couple things. It's important to be able to assess a situation and to make good prices given what's going on in the market and also the particular customer that's involved in the transactions. This comes with experience. Good traders don't crack under pressure but are able to think clearly and make the right decision, regardless of how much money they're making or losing. A good trader balances his need to make money with the interests of the customer.

**Q: What do you enjoy most about the business?**

It's a fast-paced environment and there's always something going on. I enjoy the challenge of thinking fast on my feet, pricing securities and making markets. Every day we start with nothing except our wits and enthusiasm, and it's our job to consistently make a profit. The trading environment is the closest thing to a true meritocracy that you'll ever find on Wall Street, and it's good to know that if I do a good job and make money for the firm, I'll be compensated accordingly.

**Q: What's the worst part about your job?**

We always eat lunch at our desk, and it's my responsibility to place the order and to pick up the food. Enterprising trading analysts always keep a stash of menus – you can never have enough lunch options, and traders appreciate variety. Sometimes I think that I didn't sign up to be an overpaid lunch delivery boy, but it's all part of the process and everyone has to pay their dues. Sales-traders also eat their lunch at the desk, but they're a little less harried and can afford to take a little more time with the menus, since there's normally a lull in trading activity. Traders, however, can't afford to take their eyes off the screen, since even over the lunch time lull, prices are fluctuating.

**Q: What happens to the trading analyst that just can't make it?**
Trading is a meritocracy and you are only given responsibility commensurate with your ability to get the job done. Unsuccessful analysts generally are not given the same opportunities to trade as successful analysts, and typically at the end of the two-year program, if they haven't been able to provide a value proposition to the desk, then they're not hired on a full-time basis.

# Inventory

In a retail business, inventory refers to the quantity of a product (shoes, pants soccer balls, etc.) on-hand and available for sale. Inventory in the trading business refers to positions of stock that the trader has accumulated throughout the trading day. The ideal situation is that the trader matches buyer and seller and collects a spread by buying low and selling high. For example, if he buys 100,000 shares of POS at $20 and can immediately sell the shares to another buyer at $20.06, he has made a riskless profit of $60,000 for the firm. The problem is that matching buying and seller is only an ideal situation – it is in fact is one of the hardest things to do. Buyers always have company, and sellers are never alone either. So, the trader is forced to earn his keep. He does this by adding to or selling from his inventory. The markets fluctuate, so the risk for the trader is that he buys a lot of stock when the markets are up, and for some unexpected reason later in the day, the markets go into a freefall. The trader is now losing his shirt because the inventory he purchased in the morning is getting crushed.

Traders are not investors. If the trader is long 100,000 shares (has 100,000 shares in his inventory) down 50 cents a share, he's already down $50,000 and needs to make some really tough risk management decisions. The trader does not have the luxury to say, "Well, I think the stock is fundamentally a great story, and while it may be down today, I have confidence that in six months, the stock will recover." This is all hogwash from a trader's perspective, who feasts and starves on the daily tick chart.

Should the trader sell the stock for a loss? If so, then what are the chances that he can later sell an even greater slug of stock to the customer that sold to him in the first place? This may not sound like a very attractive option, but aggressive traders have a knack for snatching victory from the jaws of defeat. One strategy is to get out there and keep buying the stock in anticipation that the seller has more stock for sale, and will be anxious to continue making sales to keep up with volume. This is called "taking the stock down to a level where it will trade." A trader would follow this strategy if he senses that a large investor, say, Fidelity, is trying to change its position in a stock and either buy up a bunch of it or unload it without being overly concerned with small price changes. In the case discussed where the trader has 100,000 shares and is down 50 cents a share, he would be betting that Fidelity will continue to sell the stock, even if the price drops, so he's buying up shares to sell back to the firm.

When the trader takes the stock down another $1, he's now losing $150,000 on his inventory. He may have sold some stock down the way, but normally if you hit the Street with enough shares (offer to buy many shares), other dealers get out of the way pretty quickly, and the price tumbles with very few prints (trades). At this point, the trader gets on the phone and tells the salesperson to call the buy-side trader (Fidelity, in our example). The salesperson puts on a panicky tone and says something like, "Joe, this stock just got creamed. I don't know who hit it, but it wasn't us and it's for sale everywhere. You want to make some sales here?" Joe is going to be pissed that the stock tumbled without getting any notice from the salesperson. The salesperson will say that the stock crumbled with no shares printing (trading), probably because there's another seller out there. Several factors will determine how much stock (if any) the buy-side trader will sell. These factors include: the portfolio manager's (also called the "PM," this is the person at the buy-side firm responsible for managing the money) instructions (does he have an ultimate low or is this a get-me-out-at-any-price type order), the relationship between the buy-side trader and the salesperson, and perhaps most importantly, the VWAP.

Buy-side traders continually track something called the volume-weighted average price, or the VWAP. The VWAP is essentially a running average share price of the stock throughout the day. Buy-side-traders (traders who work for investment management firms) who are buying want to be as far below the VWAP as possible, and sell-side traders (who work for investment banks) try to be above the VWAP. In the context of our example, if the buy-side trader can sell shares at these low prices without totally wrecking his personal VWAP (i.e., making his average selling price lower than the prevailing VWAP), then he will do it. He's also more likely to make the sale toward the end of the trading day. At the beginning of the day, sellers can be reluctant because the VWAP can change more rapidly when there's less volume on the tape and more time for the stock to trade. If the buy-side trader sells enough stock at these low prices, the salesperson happily buys the stock and banks the sales credit. The buy-side trader can report a good VWAP to his portfolio manager and the trader has the comfort of knowing that he crushed the stock and that as long as no one else tries to do the same thing, the shares should recover and he can at least break even on the trade.

This is just one example of how traders need to manage their inventory. In reality, trading is a game with infinite possibilities. What if the trader pounds the stock, buys another 100,000 shares and then some malevolent dealer decides to whack the stock (sell the stock and drive the price even lower) to inflict pain on a competitor? What if pounding the stock gets another seller in the door, and now the trader has to accommodate multiple sellers while he's lugging a huge position? What if the seller doesn't want to sell any stock down at these prices? Then all the trader has done is caused himself a nice big loss. The adept trader is one who learns from experience. He needs to understand the customer he's working with, and each firm's biases. He also needs to understand the short-term supply and demand picture of the stock. If he believes that he's the only seller in the market, but then a multitude of sellers materialize out of the woodwork, he has made a critical error in judgment. Finally, he needs to understand the capabilities of the salesperson, and the type of relationship the salesperson has with the customer. While the bid-ask spread is supposed to protect the trader, in extreme circumstances this spread offers only modest protection at best. The trader needs to have good instincts and the ability to assimilate a lot of information to make a timely decision on price and quantity that gives him a fighting chance.

## Tracking the trades

Traders buy and sell millions of shares a day, and it's the trading assistant's responsibility to insure that the P&L (profit and loss) and the positions are correct. P&L is tracked on a daily, monthly and yearly basis through firm's automated systems. Traders become particularly protective of their P&L towards the end of every month. Woe to the trading assistant who ignores an error in the accounting of the trades, called a "trade break." A trade break occurs when the two sides of a trade settle up on their trades at the end of the day, based on notes that the trading assistant has taken, and find that they don't agree on what the trade was. (Remember, the action is fast and furious, and there is a lot of trading going on constantly, not to mention yelling and other commotion.) For example, the two sides may not agree on the price or volume of a trade.

The worst kind of trade break is the "DK" or "don't know." This happens when one side of the trade goes out to the other side of the trade to settle, but the other side does not know the trade – doesn't acknowledge that an agreement was made. If it's a trade with the Street that's being DK'ed, a common mistake is that the assistant has tried to settle with the wrong dealer. Dealer trades that aren't picked up within a few hours should be investigated very promptly – if you leave it until the next day, you will very likely not be able to know the trade. Position breaks are deadly because if you have a 20,000 share purchase that needs to be busted, then all of a sudden, instead of being flat, your trader is now short 20,000 shares. If you put the trade in on the wrong side, then you're in a world of hurt, since your position will now be short 40,000 shares. As a trading assistant, you must make sure you stay on top of trade breaks. A good sign of trouble is the P&L. If you made $20,000 yesterday and your P&L shows you down $30,000, then there's a good chance that one or several of your positions are incorrect.

Perhaps less frightening is the possibility that you or the customer has a wrong average price on the trade. To pre-empt this problem, you should confirm prices with the salesperson who did the trade at the end of every day (and also do a running recap throughout the day). Don't let differences of a few cents here and there slide. Being a penny off on a one million share trade is a $10,000 error.

## Trader Talk

Trading is a lot like waging war. Traders try to protect their profits while inflicting harm on their competitors and working with their allies (the salespeople) to win major objectives (the client order). Like soldiers, traders and salespeople also have terse conversations that are laced with jargon. If you're unfamiliar with this lingo, then you probably won't have any clue what's going on when watching a trading desk in action. For this reason, new analysts and associates often struggle for weeks just to get a clue. What follows is a description of some of the most widely used jargon that you'll hear on the trading desk. This will give you a jumpstart on your first job in the industry.

**"I'm going long."**
When a trader is going long, this means that he's buying shares of stock and makes money when the stock price rises. If a trader is buying a lot of stock, he may say,"I'm going long and backing up the truck." This means the trader is buying a lot of stock because it's at a level that he thinks is favorable, and he'd like to buy as much stock as possible.

**"I'm going short."**
When a trader goes short, this means he's selling stock without actually owning it. He'll eventually cover the position (buy the stock), at which time he will say that he's flat.

**"How do you stand?"**
Salespeople will ask traders "how they stand" throughout a customer trade. For example, if the salesperson and trader have taken a customer out of 1 million shares of stock and complete the order, the salesperson may then ask the trader "How do you stand?" to get the trader's position. It's implicit that the salesperson will not pass this information along to the seller. Normally this is an unnecessary question, since the trader's position can be displayed on the internal position monitors, but some desks disable this function for salespeople, to prevent them from playing stock market with the trader's positions. (A salesperson does not know the nuances of the market for a stock. If, for example, he knows that the trader is long a stock, he may believe he is doing the trader a favor by selling it, without knowing that there is a reason the trader is keeping the inventory.) To be sure that the salesperson is not misusing this information by passing it along to the customer, the salesperson may add something like, "Just me asking."

**"I'm flat."**
The trader with no position in the stock is flat. Being flat is the best place to be at the end of the day. Sometimes, a suspicious salesperson thinks a trader has gone ahead and sold stock "ahead of a customer" and will ask the trader how he stands. (Getting stock sold or bought "ahead" of you means someone beats you to the trade. In this example, a salesperson may suspect that the trader sold stock through an

electronic network before allowing a client to buy it through the salesperson.) The most common answer to this question is "I'm flat," which communicates that the trader hasn't done anything unsavory.

### "I'm hitting the bid."

This is always a source of confusion for neophytes. The bid is the price on the left and the ask is the price on the right. The bid is the price that the dealer is willing to buy at and the offer is the price that he's willing to sell at. To "hit the bid" means you're going to sell to the dealer at his indicated bid price. If the bid size is less than your total order size, then after the displayed quantity is filled, the bid will go down.

### "I'm taking the offer."

To "take the offer" or to "lift the offer" means you're going to buy from the dealer at his indicated offering price. If your order size exceeds the displayed offering size, then after the displayed quantity is executed, the balance of your order will cause the offering price to increase. Don't confuse the bid and the ask prices. If someone tells you to hit the stock (sell the stock – remember, you'll end up taking the stock price down) and you go out and bid every dealer for stock, you're going to have a problem. To say that "I'm going to take the bid" or "I'm going to hit the offer" is an improper use of trading terminology and could earn you several undesirable nicknames.

### "I plugged him."

Traders like to be tough guys. This mafia-inspired lingo refers to a situation where another trader bids you (offers to buy) some quantity of shares and our offering dealer sells him the entire volume of what he's bidding for (offering to buy). Normally dealers won't sell more than their display size, but if the offering dealer happens to be making a stand in the stock or is working a customer order, then he's going to stand on the offering and "plug the bidding dealer" (e.g., "He bid me for 10,000 shares and I plugged him").

### "I faded him."

Fading another dealer means that the bidding dealer bought all the stock that he got hit with (bought). If a dealer has stock for sale or is trying to get the price of the stock down, he may have to go out on the street and hit dealers with a "good slug of stock." Normally, if you hit a dealer with enough stock (offer to sell a bunch of stock), the bidding dealer will buy the minimum quantity and adjust his bid price lower (also known as "getting out of the way.") If instead, the bidding dealer buys all the stock that was thrown at him, he is standing firm on the bid and is said to have "faded" the other guy.

### "That guy just backed away."

Dealers are continuously posting and updating their quotes. If a dealer fails to provide a trade at his bid or offer, then he has backed away from his quote. Backing away is essentially false advertising in trading. If a dealer shows a market and fails to honor the market, then he has basically sold the rest of the Street a false bill of goods. Often in fast-moving markets, dealers will accuse each other of backing away, when in fact a customer or competitor was able to beat the dealer to the bid or offer. In this case the dealer being accused of backing away may indicate "customer ahead" or "competitor ahead," in order to explain why he is no longer honoring the market he advertised.

### "Give me a name."

When stocks are surging or getting crushed, it's often because a dealer is moving the stock. If a salesperson is working an order with a trader, the salesperson will ask to know why the stock price is moving so much. The trader may shrug his shoulders and say "someone's hitting the stock." The salesperson will then ask the trader to "give him a name." This is necessary information for the salesperson to report back to the customer. If the stock gets hit and his trader can't make any sales, then at the very least the salesperson wants to be able to tell him who's crushing the stock.

### "I'm out there with him."

Sometimes traders are working orders for which they know that the customer is going to expect to have bought or sold some stock, even if the stock price is in motion. If the trader gets hit by another dealer (gets an offer to buy from a dealer), this is like a tripwire. The trader will bark the selling dealer's name to the salesperson and then growl "I'm out there with him," meaning that the trader will also take a whack at the stock (advertise that he wants to sell the stock). Even though he doesn't sell anything, at least he'll be able to get a lower price on the stock he's going to have to buy from the customer.

### "That was a fast call (or bad call or pickoff call)"

A fast call is the derisive term for an account that picks off the firm's trader on a regular basis. Generally, if the account calls up when the price is moving up (or down) quickly and tries to buy (or sell) a nuisance of a quantity (i.e., five or ten thousand shares), the trader calls the account a fast call. Salespeople who have too many fast call accounts tend to have poor working relationships with the firm's traders. A fast call is never a good call.

### "This knucklehead is locking the market."

Market makers are responsible for maintaining orderly markets. Part of this responsibility is to maintain a quote that does not "lock the market." The bid price is the price at which the dealer is willing to buy stock, and the selling price is the price at which the dealer is willing to sell stock. Dealers are in the business of making money, so it should always be the case that the bid price is below the offering price. A locked market looks like this:

ORCL    11.12 – 11.12

If the bid price matches the ask price, the market is locked and theoretically a buyer or seller could transact without paying the bid-ask spread (the implied cost of trading which equals the offering price minus the bid price). Dealers are always playing games with each other, but locking or crossing the market is unacceptable conduct, even for traders.

### "This #$@$! is crossing the market."

Crossing the market is when the bid price actually exceeds the ask price. Getting back to our ORCL example, a crossed market would look something like this:

ORCL    11.18 – 11.12

Theoretically, in this situation, a customer could hit the 18 cent bid and take the 12 cent offer and make a riskless 6 cent profit per share. Crossing the market is normally done if the person on the bid or offer does not respond to repeated bids or offers – the trader crosses the market to get the non-responsive dealer's attention. If no warning shots have been fired, so to speak, then crossing the market is highly unacceptable conduct. Traders can be fined for crossing or locking the market.

### "I'm real" or "I'm natural".

Traders are always playing games in the market to confuse competitors and to try and gain access to customer orders. The way to attract business is to bid or offer stock aggressively. Pizza restaurants offer "buy one get one free" offers to get new patrons in the door. Similarly, traders can bid and offer insane quantities of stock to hook into a customer order. Typically, in response to a trader's aggressive market, a client will call and ask what's going on. The client may be trying to sell stock and may have been doing so at a competing firm. At this point, the client will want to know if the trader is "real" or not. If the trader says that he is "real," it means that he's representing a customer bid. If the trader is "not real" (or says, "it's just me"), then the trader is bidding around with the firm's capital, and does not yet have the opposite side of the trade that the seller is looking for. Sellers will normally not be excited to hit a trader's bid, because once the trader buys that first piece of stock everyone sees a big chunk of stock on the bid and it's not too long before it's a panic for the exit. A natural buyer, on the other hand, presents an opportunity for the seller to unload his position with minimal disruption to the stock price. There is also the possibility that both the buyer and the seller will expand their order sizes.

**"I'm working."**

Orders that institutional customers leave for the trader to work over the course of the day are called working orders. If the client is trying to sell 100,000 shares of a stock that trades 7,000 shares a day, the normal protocol calls for the trader to execute a small portion of the order and the client will then leave the balance of the order on the desk for the trader to "work." It's important to note that working orders have to be earned. If the seller is trying to sell 1 million shares, you as the trader can't just hit all the bids and say, "Thanks, I'll call you back." The seller sees the bids disappearing and it's very obvious to everyone what you're doing. You have to make a bid on a piece of the order and if that bid is hit, then you earn the right to work the order. More nettlesome clients will try and micromanage the orders. Working orders can be market orders (where the client tells the dealer to simply execute the orders at market prices), but more often than not they're market orders with strict limits. For example, the seller may have the following instructions, "Make sales in here, but I don't want to lose stock below $25." Other times the seller may say, "I need to make sales, I'm in your hands." The second set of instructions appears to be giving more freedom for the trader to operate, but in fact it's a very mixed blessing. If the client says that he's in your hands, then the nettlesome client can be more inclined to complain about every print (execution) that you provide. On the other hand, if the seller gives you an ultimate low limit and stock doesn't trade, then you can turn the limit back on the seller's head and say that a limited quantity of stock traded above $25. Of course, the tape of the market activity that day better tell the same story.

Traders giving a report back to the salesperson will say something like, "You sold 25,000 shares at $11.12, and I'm working the balance in here."

**"I'm crossing 500,000 shares 24.02 – 24.08."**

This is the moment every trader lives for. He has a customer buyer who wants to buy the stock at 24.08 and a customer seller who wants to sell the stock at 24.02, so the trader collects 6 cents on 500,000 shares (and the salesperson gets his sales credits) without committing a penny of the firm's capital. Often, if the trader is working a seller out of his last piece of stock, then buyers will appear out of the woodwork. Nobody wants to step in front of a freight train, but if the seller has been selling persistently and is completing his order with the last trade, then the trader will often want to keep some shares in his own inventory, in anticipation of the stock price increasing ("doing better") after the seller stops leaning on the stock.

**"Can I get in on that print?"**
With large block trades, the trader needs to make sure that he doesn't step on anyone's toes. Before executing the trade, the trader will tell the salespeople what his situation is, and will give them the courtesy of making calls to their customers as a heads up. If the trader is cleaning up the seller (buying the seller's last portions of stock), then other buyers will call up frantically trying to get involved (i.e., trying to "get in on that print.") If the trader is cleaning up a buyer, then other sellers will want to get involved. This is Murphy's law of trading. The worst situation for the trader is if he takes a seller out of his last piece of stock and customers are demanding more stock than he has for sale, forcing the trader to go short a stock that everyone knows has no place to go but up.

**"The bonds traded away."**
The opposite of winning a customer trade is to have the "bonds trade away" at another dealer. Often, dealers will be asked to bid competitively against other dealers. The buy-side seller will ask for three bids in competition, and will sell to the highest bidder. Generally speaking, traders don't like this kind of treatment from their customers, and occasionally (or frequently), the trader will "bid to miss." This means the trader goes along with the game and furnishes a seemingly respectable bid which he knows the seller will not hit.

**"I'm getting pennied"**
It used to be that stocks traded in eigths, sixteenths and even thirty-seconds of a dollar. If there was a sizeable bid at 1/8ths, a trader seeking to buy the stock immediately could step in front of this bid by paying 3/16ths or ¼. With the decimalization of the market, the minimum increase or decrease in a bid or offer is now one penny. If a large bid is indicated at 12 cents, anxious traders can now place a 13 cent bid (rather than an 18 cent or 25 cent bid) which will have higher

order priority than the 12 cent bid. The trader trying to buy stock at 12 cents who loses out to a dealer buying at 13 cents will say "I just got pennied." If this happens all day long, he'll probably say something like, "I'm getting pennied to death." Trading for pennies means that the small investors can get better prices for his trade, but the bad news is that this system is also subject to manipulation by specialists who can "step ahead" of a displayed customer order by improving on the existing bid or offer by one penny.

The practice of a specialist stepping ahead of the customer and taking away the customer's trade is called "front-running." This practice is illegal; the current investigation into specialist firm trading activities centers on this alleged practice.

# The Power of Information

A trader is not only constantly refining his instincts, but is also constantly seeking to recalibrate his view of the market with information from a variety of sources. The most valuable source of information is customer order flow. Institutional traders execute huge trades for customers. Due to the size of these orders, they can exert significant influence on a stock's price. The trader always tries to stay ahead of a large order. If he has an order in hand, then the exercise is to sell as much stock as possible – the trader should be hitting every possible bid so that he will be in position to purchase more stock from his sellers. If the trader doesn't have an order, but knows that the seller was working an order to sell shares at the current market price about a week ago, then the trader is keeping bids in front of the customer (through the salesperson), to entice the customer to come back with more stock for sale. Dealers will often sell anonymously through floor brokers or electronic crossing networks to camouflage their identities. There's a lot of smoke and mirrors involved in working a customer order, so just be aware that not all things may be as they appear. For example, skilled traders are often able to create the impression of a buyer in the marketplace (even as they're quietly trying to sell stock), in an attempt to lure another dealer into bidding the stock.

Even with the information available through Bloombergs and other sources, no dealer ever has a full picture of the market. As stocks trade throughout the day, different customers and dealers are getting involved in the market. You may be sitting on an order to sell one million shares of stock, which indicates to you that the stock is headed lower. Then all of a sudden, bids start appearing fast and furious because your competitor has an order to buy two million shares. Now you're no longer the axe in in the game (the trader leading the market), and there's a good chance that you'll lose your seller to your competitor.

## The Trader's Cockpit

It costs $50,000 in computers and market data screens to equip a trader. If you've ever visited a trading desk, you may have been dazzled by the mass of technology assembled on a trader's desk. Each trader utilizes different information sources, but typically you'll find the following:

### The Bloomberg

The Bloomberg machine is ubiquitous on trading desks. It is a proprietary financial database that supports advanced financial analytics. On equity desks, Bloomberg machines are nice to have but don't really add too much value. On fixed income desks, however, the advanced analytics provided by Bloombergs are a necessary part of pricing bonds. For example, the Bloomberg can quickly calculate the amount of accrued interest due on a bond trade, and can be used to perform option-adjusted spread analysis. If you are in school, especially business school, and your library has a subscription to Bloomberg, then it's probably a good idea to try and sign up for a training session while you're at school, so that you're familiar with some of the advanced analytics capabilities of the platform.

### Phone monitor

The phone system takes a while to get used to. If you're a sales assistant, this is actually going to be one of the first things you should learn. It's okay to accidentally hang up on accounts for the first week or so, but if you're still incompetent with the phone system after a couple of weeks, you're probably not going to last long. As a trading assistant, one of the best things you can do to add value when you have no clue of what's going on is to become a secretary. Pick up the phone, ask who's calling and put the call on hold. Then, yell across the room and tell Jerry that he's got a call on whatever line that's blinking. Wait a few seconds and if the line is still blinking, yell louder. Do this when the market is opening and when the market is closing, since this is when traders and salespeople are the busiest and don't have the time to pick up the phones.

The phone display has multiple screens, so part of the learning curve is figuring out which lines are more important than others. Generally speaking, you want to pick up the regional offices. If you have salespeople in San Francisco calling, they're probably calling because they have an order or are working an order, so don't let that one blink very long. There are trading lines and sales lines. Generally the rule here is (with the exception of picking up regional offices), traders don't pick up the sales lines and the salespeople don't pick up trading lines. A salesperson's worst nightmare is a trader talking directly to his accounts, and a trader dreads the prospect of a salesperson buying or selling stock with no idea of what's happening in the market. The absolute last priority is the dealer lights (dealers are other sell-side traders). If dealers are calling, it's generally not for a good reason, so there's no rush to pick them up. You can be sure that they'll repay the favor.

### Execution platform or smaller broker screens

Bond desks have smaller green-glowing Cantor Fitzgerald broker screens, where market prices and size of markets are updated continuously. Equity desks have a variety of execution platforms called electronic crossing networks (ECN): Goldman's ECN is called Archipelago, Spear Leads' ECN is called REDI (Goldman recently acquired Spear Leads), and Bloomberg has its own trade book ECN. The common equipment that you'll find on every equity dealer's desk is an Instinet terminal. Instinet is a unit of Reuters, and Instinet did for equities what Cantor Fitzgerald did for the bond market, whcih is allow dealers to see quotes and trade through their computers rather than over the phone. Instinet's screen-based equity trading system provides anonymous liquidity to customers and dealers. Instinet is the broker's broker – before competition from ECNs and the recent market downturn, it was able to generate substantial trading revenues on an agency basis.

### Sun workstation

The Sun workstation will normally display a number of different screens customized by the trader. Traders will normally have a news ticker, an internal research notes page, a real-time tick chart of the stock index and bond futures, a carpet of other tickers representative of a sector of the market that the trader cares about, other market data pages, and a real-time position monitor that updates positions, profit and loss. The tick-chart tracks the intra-day price of a major market index, like the

Treasury-bond futures. Most investors look at weekly, monthly or yearly price charts. Traders are looking at tick charts that update every couple of seconds with every trade. If the tick chart isn't working or is delayed, this can be a major problem for the trader, since he is reacting to stale prices. As an assistant, make sure that the tick chart is updating properly! One more word of warning: if you are a trading assistant and happen to be sitting in a trader's seat, do not go ahead and customize the page. There's a reason a trader has laid out the screen as he has. Upon his return, he will not be happy spending time reorganizing his screen because a junior trader screwed it up.

# Prime Brokerage

A prime broker is designated by the client to process and settle trades that the client executes across the Street. The prime broker also maintains custody of the client's portfolio. Prime brokerage has evolved from the stock loan department. Stock loan departments have traditionally been a very attractive business. Stock loan professionals locate the borrow on behalf of clients that are interested in shorting securities. The stock loan department generate revenues by charging an appropriate rate of borrow which it passes along to the stock lender-net of the haircut that it is entitled to for its services.

Prime brokerage departments are also involved in fund administration. Fund administration is basically all the accounting and record-keeping that is anathema (but necessary) to the small-scale hedge fund operator who doesn't have the scale to keep these capabilities in-house. Some of the administration services that are offered by prime brokers include: maintaining detailed trading records, generation of performance attribution reports for tax and financial reporting purposes, calculating net asset value, multi-currency fund accounting and other corporate services. Generally speaking, access to these prime brokerage services are provided free of charge, but in return, it is expected that the hedge fund client will direct a minimum percentage of its business towards the prime broker's trading desks. There is no free lunch on Wall Street.

Working on a prime brokerage desk doesn't have the same thrill of a trading desk. The pace is lower, and there is a much higher degree of client-focus. However, this is a highly profitable business unit within the typical equity trading department-the business is relatively stable and requires a minimum amount of risk capital.

# Decrease your T/NJ Ratio
## (Time to New Job)

Use the Internet's most targeted job search tools for finance professionals.

## Vault Finance Job Board

The most comprehensive and convenient job board for finance professionals. Target your search by area of finance, function, and experience level, and find the job openings that you want. No surfing required.

## VaultMatch Resume Database

Vault takes match-making to the next level: post your resume and customize your search by area of finance, experience and more. We'll match job listings with your interests and criteria and e-mail them directly to your inbox.

# The Salespeople

## CHAPTER 3

If you're interested in sales, you may have skipped over the chapter on trading. Why should I be interested in trading if I was born to sell? If so, we strongly advise that you backtrack and read the previous chapter. We've mentioned it before, but it's worth mentioning again: sales and trading are very tightly integrated functions. Traders would be trading with themselves without salespeople, and salespeople would be losing their shirts buying millions of shares from fast customers without traders. Good traders are also good salespeople, and good salespeople need to have a good idea of what traders are thinking. Of course, no trader wants a salesperson telling him what the right price for a trade is, and salespeople don't appreciate traders ramming a price down their client's throat either, but a mutual understanding of each other's requirements facilitates transactions and, in theory at least, should increase profitability.

## Brokers No Longer

Bud Fox of *Wall Street* fame was a broker. Today, the broker title is eschewed and we have two broad categories of salespeople: institutional salespeople and private client services (PCS) professionals. Institutional salespeople cover large institutional firms. These firms include mutual funds, public pension funds, insurance companies and trust organizations. PCS professionals cater to wealthy individuals.

### Institutional salespeople

Broadly speaking, there are two types of institutional sales professionals: the sales-trader and the research salesperson. A sales-trader sits on the sales and trading desk and acts as the interface between the client organization (the buy-side firm) and the broker-dealer organization (the investment bank or specialist trading firm). The sales-trader speaks directly with the buy-side traders.

A research salesperson sells the firm's research to the buy-side organizations, and speaks directly with portfolio managers and analysts. The research salesperson tries to convince the portfolio manager and analysts to use his firm's research analysts and reports to assist in the investment decision process. Sell-side firms are ranked annually on the quality of their research, and there tends to be a correlation between the amount of business a research salesperson is able to generate for the firm, and the perceived quality of his firm's research analysts. Both the sales-trader and the research salesperson are heavily involved in building client relationships. While this obviously includes quality execution and useful research, salespeople also frequently take clients out for industry conferences and golf outings in an effort to strengthen their relationships with clients, with the idea that this will result in more commission dollars.

## Private client services professionals (PCS)

The other breed of salesperson is the private client services professional (PCS). PCS professionals cover wealthy individuals. Certain organizations like Goldman Sachs pursue a regional coverage strategy, so that if you're selling equities in Dallas, you can only cover clients within this region. Other firms, like Bear Stearns, pursue a more opportunistic coverage strategy: cover anyone, anywhere. If you are interested in PCS, it's worth finding out what type of coverage strategy the firm employs.

## The difference between the two

There are several key points of difference between institutional sales and PCS. First, institutional sales is a bit more glamorous. At a cocktail party, it sounds a little more refined to say that you cover a known institution rather than an assortment of wealthy dot-com millionaires who day-trade in their spare time. On the other hand, on a per-share basis, PCS is a much higher margin business. PCS salespeople are often able to charge a significantly higher commission than their institutional sales counterparts, especially if the client values the relationship with the PCS professional. PCS is also a little more interesting from the perspective that the potential client base is always changing. At one point in *Wall Street*, Bud Fox's boss hands him a thick telephone directory, reminding him that, "There are plenty of six-figure prospects that you should be cold-calling." When you get down to it, this is essentially how a new PCS professional builds his book of business. There are occasional new client opportunities that surface, but there is a lot of pitching and cold-calling involved even before the first trade can be traded. While investment banking analysts put together pitchbooks ad nauseum, PCS professionals cold-call ad nauseum, often getting hung up on several hundred times a day.

Institutional sales is a more structured environment in the sense that there is less cold-calling involved in the job description. The institutional business is more of a zero-sum game. There are only, say, 100 top worldwide accounts that every firm is focused on covering (although there is a middle-market business that caters to firms that are a little bit under the radar in terms of assets under management.) By and large, institutional salespeople are literally out to eat each other's lunch. While there's an offensive component to institutional sales, at top firms at least, a lot of what goes on is playing defense. The successful institutional salesperson stays on top of his game by keeping his clients happy, and not doing anything that could jeopardize the long-term client relationship. The worst thing that can happen to a salesperson is to have his or her share of that client's business dwindle, since building that business back up takes a lot of time and money. Institutional commissions on a per-share-transacted basis are substantially lower than in the PCS world, but institutional salespeople will always say that it's a volume business, and what they don't make in fat spreads, they make back on volume. Trading a million shares for a few pennies a share still adds up to a few million pennies.

# What Makes a Good Salesperson?

Above all, a good salesperson needs to have a passion for the markets. In your interviews, you also need to demonstrate a passion for selling (of course, prior market experience is a big plus). Once you're hired and have landed your sales job, you'll pick up the skills you need to succeed. Typically, if you're sitting on an institutional sales desk, you'll begin by listening in on client calls. There is a button on the headset that mutes you out of the conversation, and you can listen in on any conversation unobtrusively. On these calls, you'll learn the language of the business and the different styles of different salespeople. You'll also get a sense of what different types of clients expect – and the Golden Rule in sales on Wall Street is to always know your client.

Eventually, you'll get to the point where you have an opportunity to cover your own accounts. Don't expect to be covering Fidelity or Alliance any time soon. You'll typically be assigned some low-activity middle-market accounts, often in out-of-the-way places. From the perspective of your employer, this is a chance for you to build up a book of business, and it's relatively low-risk – if you blow up the account, it doesn't really matter much to the bottom line, since the account wasn't doing much business anyway. With these accounts, you practice delivering the morning research call and developing a bona fide sales relationship with the account. If you're capable and lucky, several of these accounts will generate meaningful revenues, and you may soon find yourself in contention to cover some of the larger accounts at the firm. Most dealers have very comprehensive commission runs (the sales credits the salesperson gets) and rank the largest buy-side customers by shares traded and profitability. As your influence grows, you'll be covering firms closer to the top of the list. Recognize again, though, that this is a zero-sum game, and that really the only way that you'll be able to break into these top accounts is through persistent efforts, meaningful profitability and a little luck. On the bright side, turnover on the Street is significant, so if you're doing all these things and are in the right place at the right time, eventually you may find yourself landing a large account (a.k.a. "bagging the elephant").

The process for building a business in PCS sales is similar. After your training, you'll start by cold-calling a list of qualified prospects. "Qualified prospects" sound promising, but in reality you could be cold-calling for weeks at a time before someone is willing to give you the time of day. If you're able to line up a few meetings with prospects, then most firms will send you along with a more seasoned PCS professional to back you up, and to give you a sense of how veterans get the job done. Ideally, as you build your book of business, you'll learn to fly solo on these meetings, and eventually get a few big customers that are willing to give you a shot.

## Walking the fine line

Capable institutional and PCS salespeople recognize that because they are servicing both the trader and the customer, they are in a very difficult spot. If the trader is happy, this often means that the customer is not, and vice versa. Part of being a successful salesperson is developing the soft skill of knowing when to stand up for the client or the trader, and doing so in a way that maintains the long-term client relationship. For example, if a salesperson is covering a demanding top-tier account that is always asking for an adjustment on a print, this will grate on the trader, who has the responsibility of making money. (When a client asks for the terms of a trade to be modified after the fact, this is called an "adjustment on a print." For example, a client may agree to sell a certain amount of stock at a certain price, and later, after seeing the stock price run up, return and ask for a small increase in the previously agreed-upon price.) The trader of course is willing to take a few hits for the team and keep clients happy, but is certainly not in business to die by a thousand cuts. In this situation, the sales-trader needs to convince the customer that the trader is bending over backwards for him, and that continually asking for a better price is not necessary, since the trader is always putting his best foot forward. On the flip side, if a trader is constantly buying stock from a customer and the stock jumps every time the trade confirmation is given, the sales-trader needs to be able to have a conversation with the trader to make a better price for the customer. In the long run, the trader needs to make aggressive markets to the customer, so that the customer doesn't have the temptation to take his orders elsewhere. To do this, a salesperson needs to have confidence and also needs to have a thick skin. Sales-traders are often getting yelled at by traders at their firms, while also getting an earful from angry customers. This can be a rather unpleasant work environment if you take things personally.

## Know the customer and the traders

In order to walk the fine line, sales professionals need to be keenly aware of the actors involved in each trade. The sales-trader needs to know which of his accounts are good and trustworthy accounts. If a trader is working a large seller of a particular stock, and the salesperson makes the wrong call, the stock could plummet, leaving the desk with a big loss and the trader fuming over the "bad call" someone made to a fast account (a client that buys and sells opportunistically rather than reliably moving large amounts of stock through a trusting relationship with the dealer). At the same time, calls to fast customers can be exactly what the doctor ordered. Salespeople need to develop an understanding of each firm's MO, and must work to foster a high level of trust with the firm's traders. If traders suspect the ability of their salespeople, the traders may end up withholding merchandise from salespeople, opting instead to sell their merchandise to the Street (through an electronic network). While this can be done profitably, the salespeople lose out on the possibility of generating a big trade with a big customer. The trust relationship between traders and customers needs constant nurturing, and a successful salesperson doesn't lose sight of this essential fact.

## Listen to the flow of the trading desk

A pet peeve of traders is salespeople who aren't tuned into what they are trying to do. For example, say a trader gets on the firm's hoot and holler (the intercom) advertised as a seller all week. After a week of making noise and trying to get people involved, a salesperson walks over to the trader and asks what he has going on in the stock. Incredulously, the trader might say, "I'm a seller, I've been advertising myself as a seller all week!" The sales-trader grins sheepishly and says, "Can you take another 100,000 shares for sale?" Now the salesperson in this scenario has made two mistakes. First, the salesperson has apparently been totally oblivious to what the trader has been trying to do all week. Second, rather than bringing in a buyer, the salesperson has a seller, and in order to keep both sellers on the desk, the trader will end up having to buy stock from two sellers rather than one, not a particularly appetizing prospect. Of course, salespeople can't tell their customers what to do, and it's not always a bad thing to have multiple sellers on the desk, but the salesperson should have said something like, "I know you're out as a seller, but I have XYZ account in to me trying to sell stock. They saw you out on the system all week as a seller and want to go where the volume is." Now, if the salesperson says something like this, the trader feels like superman for moving the market, and even if he has to lose some money on the orders, he knows that he has a capable salesperson who is on top of his game and fully apprised of the situation that is unfolding. This may seem like a subtlety, but it makes all the world of difference in a high-pressure business.

## Q&A with an Institutional Sales-Trader at a Bulge Bracket NYC Firm

**Q: How do you prepare for the trading day?**

On the way into work, I read *The Wall Street Journal* and *Investor's Business Daily* as a way to review yesterday's market activity. I get into work around 7:00 a.m., and I'm reviewing the news and analyst notes on our firm's internal research system. The most important part of the morning for me is the morning call, when analysts give a brief summary and Q&A on the stocks where they have issued a research report. I pay particularly close attention to new initiations of coverage, upgrades and downgrades, changes in target price and the justification for these analyst actions. Research analysts love talking about EBITDA multiples and are constantly evaluating the latest technology in technical jargon that nobody understands. I need to translate lengthy analyst commentary into an understandable language for my clients. My institutional clients are inundated with calls from my counterparts at competing firms, and I strive to be the first to deliver timely market information and value-added investment research.

**Q: What is your typical routine?**

Once the call is over, I check the desk's opening indications. If I've done a big business in a particular stock, I touch base with the trader to see which way he wants to go, and what type of bid or offer I could mention to the buyer or seller just to have a conversation and to get the juices flowing early in the morning. There's a real flood of information and the most challenging part of my job is to synthesize all this data into a tight and cohesive call to my clients. Clients respond well to a sales-trader who can communicate relevant information and insights succinctly, and I'm always working to refine my communication skills, and to get to know my clients better. Even with the best call, it takes time for me to build up a relationship with my clients, and it's very important to be able to build up the trust in relationships in this business. This is particularly challenging since traders don't want to trade with customers they've never done business with, and my clients are wary of unscrupulous traders. My job is to help everyone get along.

**Q: How do you get a customer order?**

I normally will try and solicit orders before the market opens, since the traders over here appreciate working orders as early as possible. The reality is that in this game, everyone likes to keep their cards pretty close to the vest. Even if a customer's been selling stock every day for the past week, it's sometimes difficult to get this order back before the market opens, due to the aforementioned issue of trust. When the market opens up, if it's a busy day, the phones are ringing and the order flow is rolling in. 25,000 shares of XYZ in at $30 – I get a nod from the trader and write the ticket. Normally I need to get a working order, but for top-tier accounts, 25,000 shares are a cost of doing business. The trader knows that at best he's going to break-even on this trade. That's the cost of business of attracting the larger orders. Traders are giving my fills on working orders and making their 6 cents, and I'm accumulating my sales credits. Everyone has strong incentives to maximize individual measures of performance, but recognizing the centrality of the customer to everything that we do keeps everyone honest. It's unwise to sacrifice the long-term customer relationship for any one particular trade.

If, as is often the case, it's a slow day in the market, then it's a game of taking market share away from our competitors. Maybe my trader tells me that a seller's been around in Intel for the past few days, and it's our job to roll out with super messages and AUTEX trade volume. Super messages are bids or offers that the trader makes to hook into a customer order. It's basically advertising. For example, if Intel is currently trading at $15, he might make a $15 bid for 500,000 shares to attract the seller that we think is out there in the marketplace. It's a low-probability game, but in the event that our super message does attract incremental business, engaging in this activity generates incremental revenue for the firm. Regardless of the situation, I'm always asking for orders, and trying to create an obligation on the part of the customer to trade with us if and when he's ready to pull the trigger.

**Q: You referred to yourself as a sales-trader. Is there a difference between a salesperson and a sales-trader?**
Not really. OTC equity salespeople are sales-traders. Some listed equity desks also have sales-traders in addition to their block traders (who tend to transact in larger order sizes). The sales-trader is a hybrid positon – part sales and part trading. The sales-trader is responsible for initiating calls with clients. I'm constantly pitching new stock ideas and updating my clients with our research department's market commentary.

Salespeople, particularly in research sales, for example, need to be much more familiar with the details of a stock's story. Research sales are focused on selling the firm's research capabilities to institutional clients. A significant portion of any firm's research sales commissions are generated through soft dollar arrangements, where the broker agrees to kick back a portion of the commission to pay for certain client services, such as Bloomberg terminals and other subscription services.

**Q: What do you think is important for success as a sales-trader?**
This business requires the ability to communicate effectively and to tell a brief and compelling story about a company. The buy-side is inundated with sell-side calls, and being able to convince the customer that immediate action is required sounds simple enough but is very difficult to accomplish on a daily basis. The stories we're going out on are developed by our research analysts, and the market views are constantly updated by our traders. I need to stay on top of all of this and pass along the most relevant information to my clients on a real-time basis.

Beyond strong communication skills, it's really important to be able to prioritize and to multi-task. Prioritizing customers when multiple lights are ringing is important, since the best service should be delivered to the best customers. Sometimes exceptions need to be made – it's important to know which situations demand these exceptions. For example, if I've been talking to a second-tier client who happens to own a big chunk of Intel, and Intel is going wild at that particular moment in time, maybe it's better for me to pick up this customer and let my backup coverage deliver the latest fill to the top-tier account.

Multi-tasking is also very important. Trading tends to be very heavy at the opening and closing of the market, and that's when I have to be on my game. Every situation is fluid, and the price I'm quoting to the person on the other end of the phone is by definition negotiable up to the minute the transaction is relayed to the customer. The trader may be trying to adjust the price or change the quantity. At the same time, I need to be able to read my customer to discern whether or not any changes to the fill will be acceptable, or if I'll end up losing the order if I make the change. Remember, without the customer, we don't have much reason to be in this business in the first place. As the intermediary between the trader and the client, my job is to insure that everyone gets along, and that the client and firm interests are represented and balanced throughout the course of the trade.

# Q&A with a Private Client Services (PCS) Professional

## Q: What is PCS?

PCS professionals offer a complete range of financial services and products to meet the needs of high-net-worth individuals. The bare minimum is brokerage, but we also provide our clients with access to alternative investments (i.e., hedge funds and private equity funds) as well as trust, estate and tax advisory services.

## Q: How do you prepare for the trading day and what kind of hours do you work?

It's a constant dialogue with investors to help them better understand their overall asset allocation decision. Once this decision has been made, we pay a lot of attention to determining the optimal stocks and bonds to own within this portfolio. To this end, I'm always reviewing client holdings, and we're re-evaluating this investment proactively on an ongoing basis.

I work pretty standard market hours. I'm normally in around 7:30 a.m. and out around 6:00 p.m. My work is entirely client-driven, however, so this means that I'm meeting with clients for breakfast, lunch, dinner and drinks.

**Q: How do you make a customer call?**
It's best if I'm making the call proactively. To the extent that I have timely and actionable market information, my customers really appreciate the heads-up. On the other hand, if I'm making the call to sell and the stock is already down 40 percent on the day, this is a tougher conversation to have. The bottom line is that each conversation is an opportunity for me to build up my relationship with my client, and so I have to take each call seriously. It only takes one bad call to undo the goodwill built up through 10 good calls.

**Q: How do you get a customer order?**
My credibility is on the line every day. Some of my customers have given me discretionary authority over their accounts. This means that I have a lot of discretion to recommend and execute trades on behalf of my clients. Other customers prefer to make their own decisions and solicit my input as a reality check on their own decision-making process. I give my honest opinion, and consider first and foremost the suitability of the particular transaction as it relates to that particular customer. I am compensated based on commissions, but it's important to consider the long-term relationship with the account. I generate customer orders by staying current with my investors' needs and their preferences. I strive for a two-way dialogue with my customers, and make recommendations based on what my client is telling me, and what I believe are the best interests of the customer.

An emerging trend in the industry is towards managed accounts, where the firm is compensated as a percentage of assets under management rather than on a per-trade basis. This has definite implications for the quality of service that is demanded and arguably aligns the customer's long-term interest with the broker's financial interest.

**Q: What do you think is important for success as a salesperson?**
Being persistent and having a real passion for selling. The great thing about this business is that it's entirely my business to cultivate and grow. It's very entrepreneurial. The firm gives me access to all its resources and it's up to me to create a value proposition for each prospective client of the firm.

**Q: Why did you chose PCS?  Why not institutional sales?**
I enjoy working with individuals to meet their personal goals and financial needs.  PCS is a more flexible work environment where I have the potential to make a real difference in the lives of my clients.  PCS is also a more profitable business.  Institutional sales have higher volumes, but margins are always being pressured – margins are fatter and there's more financial reward per share traded.

**Q: What advice do you have for prospective PCS candidates?**
Know the differences of culture in each firm.  Different firms have different cultures, and this almost certainly will have a very significant impact on how your career develops.  Also know how much structure there is at the firm you're interested in working for.  Some places, like Bear Stearns, are incredibly entrepreneurial.  All you have to do is prospect aggressively and build a client relationship.  Other places, like Goldman Sachs, have regional coverage, and you can't cover a client in Atlanta if you're working out of the San Francisco office.  Most firms are somewhere in between these two extremes.  Know where your target firm is along this spectrum, and be comfortable with this arrangement.

**Q: What happens to the PCS professional who can't build a book of business?**
The organization is very supportive, and there's an understanding that building a business takes time.  There's a training program that familiarizes the new PCS team member about the different product areas and the resources of the firm.  Senior PCS professionals are always willing to share their wisdom with the newer members of the team.  Junior members will also do client/prospecting visits together with senior professionals to learn how to conduct a client meeting.  It also helps to build confidence.

It's pretty standard across the Street to start off with a salary and bonus plan for the first year or two.  This arrangement makes sense, since it takes time to learn the business.  After this time in training, compensation shifts to being almost entirely based on commission plus fees based on assets under management.  The bottom line is that the organization is fully supportive to a point, but eventually the PCS professional will need to produce commissions or he won't be able to be able to earn a decent living.

# Q&A with a Senior Fixed Income Salesperson

**Q: Why did you choose fixed income derivative sales?**

I found the product to be fascinating. Understanding fixed income derivatives requires an understanding of spreads, credit analysis, pricing models and other quantitative factors. There's no other product where this technical interplay is as rigorous.

**Q: How did you build your business?**

I started in an apprenticeship role, learning from senior salespeople. Eventually I had the opportunity to work with some accounts off the radar screen. I did this successfully, building my relationships from the ground up. The firm didn't have much to lose by assigning me this coverage, and potentially had a lot to gain. Happily, things have worked well for me since.

**Q: What can an undergrad or MBA student interested in sales do to develop this interest?**

Well, there's one piece of advice that I'd certainly give to aspiring salespeople: Don't claim to know something that you only have a peripheral understanding of. If you walk into an interview and claim to know duration, forward curves, skew and volatility smile, then you better believe that I'm going to ask you about it in the interview big time. There's some upside to saying you know these concepts, but be mindful of the downside.

Regarding what a candidate can do, the standard advice applies: read the paper, follow the markets and be prepared to communicate your opinions effectively. Also, remember that the most important quality that we're looking for is personality: you need to fit the job and the desk.

**Q: What is your career path?**

Eventually, successful salespeople bump up against the management level, but be ready for a long apprenticeship. The time it takes varies by individual, but it also varies by market. All things being equal, capable salespeople can expect to make big breakthroughs faster in less mature markets. As you hit your stride and build your book of business, you also are limited in terms of growing your book. There are a finite number of accounts that are looking at fixed income derivatives, so whereas early in your career you can distinguish yourself by building strong relationships, once you're established, you have to focus on growing what you have. At this point, you are constantly seeking subtle ways of distinguishing yourself.

The reality is that only one person gets to become a boss. While the sales environment is basically a meritocracy, there are always plenty of good people who deserve to get promoted. For this reason, promotions can seem pretty arbitrary, and being lucky can and often is a decisive factor.

# Financial Markets and Economics

## CHAPTER 4

## Economic Statistics

If you've ever watched CNBC on the first Friday of the month at 8:30 a.m., you've witnessed a bewildering spectacle. The scene looks something like this: a very large crowd of traders dressed in colorful outfits stand in a pit (the Chicago Board of Trade, or CBOT) waiting with bated breath for the release of the Labor Department's employment report. The number is released, and instantly, there is a surge of activity. Traders jump and yell and signal with their hands. Treasury bond futures spike, and almost instantly, the S&P 500 futures and the NDX begin dropping. Within seconds, S&P futures are locked limit down, and the S&P sellers start dumping NFX futures which had been stabilizing. These had been stabilizing but resume their freefall as a second wave of sellers swamp the market. Cash markets react to the surge in the bond futures. By 8:31 a.m., OTC equity traders react to the lower NDX futures by marking down bellweather technology stocks across the board. By 8:32 a.m., on bond desks across the Street, the firm's economist is weighing in on the number. The headline number was worse than expected, he says, but there's some good news. The previous month's unemployment rate was revised downward by a full two-tenths of a percent, and he suspects that this month's weakness is due to unseasonably cold winter weather. This blow-by-blow is repeated simultaneously across the Street, and dealers and customers begin tripping over each other trying to cover their shorts. By 8:33 a.m., the bond futures tick chart looks like an upside-down V, and bond futures fall back down to being unchanged on the day. The S&P futures recover instantly, and it's as if the whole big hullabaloo never happened. Bond futures and S&P futures are unchanged on the day, but because of the preceding flurry of activity, millions of dollars have been made and lost on the interpretation of an economic statistic – even before the stock market has opened.

Salespeople and traders need to understand economic statistics because these economic releases are potentially market-moving events. Traders need to know what statistics are coming up because this feeds into their decisions of what overnight positions can be taken. For example, if a trader happens to be long 50,000 shares of a volatile technology stock, he's going to want to know if a consumer confidence number is going to be released. If the trader is caught long 50,000 shares ahead of a big economic number and gets sandbagged, the boss is going to come over, which will be a very unpleasant way to start the morning. The trader will then turn to his assistant/junior trader and yell at him until the stock starts to show signs of life, at which time the yelling will subside. However, once the dead cat stops bouncing, the trading assistant will get another earful.

Salespeople need to know about economic statistics, because when their customers call up asking what the *&^% just happened to the futures, they need to be able to give an intelligent explanation.

The bottom line is that aspiring traders and salespeople can do themselves a big favor by learning about the different economic indicators. Easiest way to do this? Pay attention in economics class and read *The Wall Street Journal's* Money & Investing section.

## Figuring out what's important

S&T professionals are inundated with information, but the good ones always have one eye on the news ticker and can spot the important news items while trading a block of shares and picking up the intercom. This is especially true of government releases of economic statistics. The government is always releasing statistics, but you need to be able to determine what is important to the market. One way to do this while at a firm is to read some of the firm's economic research, which is always available on the in-house research notes system. Reading this research will give you some idea of what the market happens to be obsessed about at the time. Wall Street has a very short and limited attention span and tends to focus on only several indicators at any given point in time. For example, if the market is worried about inflation, then everyone focuses on the consumer price index, the producer price index and the employment cost index. If the market is concerned about a bubble in housing prices, there will be a focus on housing starts and permits. If people are concerned about weakness in manufacturing, then they look at durable goods orders, capacity utilization and the purchasing manager's index. If the market is concerned about a protracted recession, traders scruitinize weekly jobless claims and the monthly employment report. The market is always obsessed with something, so keep your eye on what the market cares most about at any given time. The bottom line is that while you don't have to become an expert economist, good traders are able to recognize set-ups that they have seen before, and position themselves accordingly.

# The Fed

If you're interested in becoming a bond trader or salesperson, you need to watch the Fed. (Any S&T professional should watch the Fed, but fixed income professionals especially should do so.) The Fed controls the money supply by changing the reserve requirement (the amount that Federal Reserve System member banks must hold in cash or on deposit with the Federal Reserve System, usually a percentage of their deposits), by conducting open market operations (buying and selling Treasuries) and most importantly, by controlling interest rates. The term "monetary policy" refers to the collective actions taken by the Fed to influence the cost of money and credit in line with national goals. It is generally acknowledged that the principal goal of the Fed is to promote price stability (i.e., combat inflation and deflation). Note that the Fed is not responsible for keep unemployment low, or to keeping the stock market buoyant, although these are certainly very desirable goals.

The Federal Open Markets Committee (FOMC) holds eight regularly scheduled meetings per year. At these meetings, the Committee reviews financial conditions throughout the economy, determines the appropriate stance of monetary policy, and assesses the risks to the economic outlook. The FOMC's policy decisions are undertaken to foster the long-term objectives of price stability and sustainable economic growth. Changes in the federal funds rate trigger a chain of events that affect other short and long-term interest rates, foreign exchange rates, and the amount of money and credit. Eventually, the economy responds with changes in employment, output, prices and the level of goods and services provided.

## Fed watching

Fed watching is an art. The Federal Reserve has typically been shrouded in mystery, and it is the job of highly paid economists and bond traders to ascertain shifts in monetary policy by watching the Fed. Economists pore over the release of the FOMC's minutes. Lately, a behavioral indicator that has come into vogue is the "Greenspan briefcase indicator." This indicator says that the thicker the briefcase Federal Reserve Chairman Alan Greenspan carries as he walks into the FOMC meeting, the more likely he is to cut rates. If the briefcase is thin, then Greenspan has very few charts and exhibits to support his proposal to cut or raise rates, so pundits expect no change in monetary policy.

S&T professionals typically focus on the change in interest rates, since open market operations are routine, and it is very rare for the Fed to change the reserve requirements. To anticipate the future course of monetary policy, traders scrutinize the flow of economic statistics. While certain figures are more important than others at any given point in time, in general, the Fed will be prompted to move in response to a series of strong or weak economic reports. A lot of money can be made by speculating on inflection points in monetary policy. There is also money to be made on the continuation or abatement of a particular monetary policy.

Traders and salespeople look at a variety of indicators, but one indicator that is pervasive is the Fed funds future. The Federal funds interest rate is the rate at which banks charge each other for the use of Federal funds; the Fed doesn't actually set this rate but effectively controls it by buying and selling Treasuries to and from other banks. (The Fed actually sets the Federal Reserve discount rate, which is the rate at which member banks may borrow short term funds directly from a Federal Reserve Bank.) Fed fund futures reflect the market's opinion on the future course of interest rates. In advance of a 2:15 p.m. Fed policy statement, you may have heard market commentators say that "the market is pricing in an 80 percent chance of a 25 basis point cut in interest rates by the Fed." How can this market opinion be quantified? Let's assume that the current Fed Funds rate is 3 percent, and that we are in the month of February. The March Fed Fund futures are trading at 2.80 percent (let's ignore the cost of carry). 2.80 percent is 20 basis points (bps) below the current Fed Funds rate (100 basis points equals 1 percent). This means that the market is expecting the Fed Funds rate to be cut by 20 bps, or 80 percent of 25 bps (the Fed normally moves in increments or multiples of 25 bps).

# Which Indicator?

There are certain economic statistics that just never seem to generate much attention. This can occur for several reasons. Sometimes the data that is being released is so old that it's already old news. Economists have a fancy term for this, it's called a "lagging indicator." One such example is construction spending. This data is released on the first business day of the month for the two months prior. By this time, the market has already digested housing starts and new and existing home sales, and could care less about what happened two months ago. Another example is business inventories. Business inventories are an important component of GDP, but the markets tend to ignore business inventory releases. As with the construction spending data, business inventory releases are preceded by retail sales, factory orders and a whole slew of other data points that gives us important clues into how inventories are shaping up. The market is always forward looking.

Other indicators, such as the trade balance are just too abstruse. Traders have limited attention spans, and can deal with monthly revisions, but concepts like the trade balance are just too wishy-washy. The trade balance is calculated as net exports. But the problem is that there's a lot that's open for interpretation. For example, if the trade deficit comes in narrower than expected, then bond traders must contend with two conflicting and opposite factors. A narrow trade deficit is good for the dollar, since fewer import producers will be selling dollars. On the other hand, a narrower trade deficit means a higher net exports figure which is accretive to GDP and bad for bonds. Unlike most other indicators which are either good or bad, the trade deficit is often pretty mixed. Enterprising economists will try and decipher the trade deficit, but this generally produces a collective yawn from the firm's bond traders.

Although some indicators are not widely watched, many market mavens try and simplify economic release data by focusing on one or two "magic bullets." This is a very flawed methodology. As mentioned previously, different market conditions create anxiety and concern over different economic indicators, so the skilled trader needs to know what the market cares about at any given time and focus his efforts accordingly.

## Gauging market reaction to economic indicator: Pricing in the news

Trying to make sense of economic indicators is tough, even for seasoned veterans. Understanding economic indicators is not just about knowing what a housing start is. The real challenge is taking into account where the market is, and how the market will react to a given indicator. For example, if the market is anticipating a lower than expected GDP report and has been selling off for four straight sessions in anticipation of this weakness, the trader doesn't look at the number and say, "Gee, that's worse than expected, just like I and everyone else expected, I better sell." The trader tries to assess the extent to which a particular market view is "priced into" the market and positions himself accordingly.

## Gauging market reaction to economic indicator: Headline risk

Sometime if you're watching a market indicator, like the Treasury bond futures, you'll see a big move either up or down followed by an equally violent move in the opposite direction in a very short period of time. This is usually the market responding to the substantive nature of the economic report.

**Economic reports are released to the newswire services showing up on your Bloomberg or another terminal at your desk. You may see something like this:**

<<NOV. CPI + 3.7%>>

Let's assume the market was expecting 2.4%, so this is really a much higher than expected consumer price index reading for November. Bonds sell off in earnest.

**Then several seconds later, the following headline comes up:**

<<NOV CPI ex food and energy + 2.1%>>

The plot thickens here, since stripping out the volatile food and energy components from the CPI reading indicates that "core" inflation has increased at a rate much lower than the initial headline number suggested. So now bonds have stopped going down and are actually starting to spike.

**Shortly after the ex food and energy headline, another headline hits the tape:**

<<OCT CPI revised down to 1.8% from 2.2%>>
<<SEPT CPI revised down to 1.7% from 2.0%>>

Now bonds are starting to rally through the roof. The downward revisions to prior months' CPI readings is the fuel that causes shorts to cover and for traders to press their long positions. The lesson here is that not only is the market continuously pricing in expectations, it is also vulnerable to wild price fluctuations when economic statistics are released. This tendency of prices to gyrate wildly in response to the headlines is called "headline risk."

| IF THIS INDICATOR GOES UP | BOND MARKET REACTION |
| --- | --- |
| GDP | Down |
| Initial jobless claims | Up |
| Payroll employment | Down |
| Unemployment rate | Up |
| Auto sales (car and truck) | Down |
| ISM purchasing managers' index | Down |
| Factory orders | Down |
| Industrial production | Down |
| Capacity utilization | Up |
| Consumer confidence | Down |
| Housing starts | Down |
| New home sales | Down |
| Producer price index | Down |
| Consumer price index | Down |
| Durable goods orders | Down |
| Retail sales | Down |
| Personal income | Down |
| Personal spending | Down |
| Leading economic indicators | Down |
| Non-farm productivity | Up |
| Unit labor costs | Down |

# The Stock Market

You may wonder how the stock market reacts to these economic indicators. First, let's remember that the stock market tends to do best when corporate earnings are increasing. This tends to happen when the economy is chugging along with minimal inflation. On the other hand, the bond market actually does best when the economy is slowing down or in a recession. To understand this, remember that bonds pay their investors a fixed rate. When the economy is in the dumps, the Fed will most likely cut interest rates, making the value of existing bonds greater (because newly issued comparable bonds will carry a lower coupon rate). Inflation is a bond investor's worst enemy, because it erodes the real return of the bond's coupon income.

Therefore, the stock market will typically move in the opposite direction as bonds.

## Earnings season

The equivalent of Fed watching for the stock market is earnings season. One of the primary responsibilities of a trading assistant is to keep a calendar marked with all the earnings release dates for the current quarter. A trading assistant's nightmare is to come into work one day and find that one of the stocks he or she covers is down $27/share. The stock actually went out yesterday at $50/share, so the market cap has been cut by more than half. The trading assistant then looks at the position monitor and notices a big position in the same stock. The trader barks at the assistant asking what the hell is going on in the stock. The assistant furiously checks through the news and finds the following headlines on Bridge (a financial news service):

<PRE-ANNOUNCES Q1 REVENUE SHORTFALL>
<CFO: ORDER SHIPMENTS FELL OFF IN THE LAST WEEK OF THE QUARTER>
<CFO: LACK OF ORDER VISIBILITY DUE TO ONGOING ECONOMIC WEAKNESS>
<REDUCING Q1 REVENUE AND EPS DOWN BY 50%>
<SUSPENDING FULL YEAR REVENUE AND EARNINGS ESTIMATES>

The trader has been blindsided, and after the trader finishes ripping into the assistant, the hapless assistant will be demoted to fetching coffee for an entire month. Don't let this happen to you. Contact firm analysts and get an idea of when each company is expected to report and what the consensus estimate is. You also need to be clear on the timing of the release. It does you no good to know that Electronic Darts (EDTS) will be releasing its number on the 27th if they report before the market opens (and you were expecting the report after the market closes). Earnings reporting calendars are also available on a number of commercial web sites – if you still can't find the date, then call the company's investor relations department.

You should also be vigilant the month before the earnings are due to be released. This is the pre-announcement season, when companies have an opportunity to confess to lower earnings and revenues ahead of the scheduled earnings release. Supposedly, it is better for the company to inform the Wall Street analyst community of a shortfall well in advance of the earnings release date. Though it may be proper etiquette, it is also a kiss of death for most companies – the stock will subsequently take a significant hit. If the trader asks you why the stock is down, you win by being the first to give him the scoop. If you are able to briefly relay to him the magnitude of the shortfall and how bad the number is, then you help your trader look good, and in the end, this can only be good for you. Get to know the firm's research analyst covering your sector, solicit his or her opinions, and be sure to pass along noteworthy information to your trader. The enterprising assistant will get in to work extra early during pre-announcement and earnings season exactly for this reason.

Not all pre-announcements are bad. Positive pre-announcements are situations where earnings are exceeding prior guidance. Again, the trading assistant should proactively gather and disseminate this information.

Be careful: stocks do not always react as expected. Sometimes stocks move up on bad news and vice versa. There can be several reasons for this, but one reason is that traders are especially aware of the situation where the news has "already been priced into the price." For example, say a firm pre-announces earnings short of expected earnings for the fifth-consecutive quarter. Perhaps it is the portfolio's manager opinion that all the bad news has been priced into the shares of the stock, and the bad news is actually good news in the sense that all the sellers will have probably already sold. Traders have much shorter time horizons, but the same logic applies. If a stock is trading down a substantial amount in the pre-opening market, then the trader may decide that at this point, the selling is overdone and that he should be bidding aggressively to catch the anticipated bounce in the share price. However, a trader may buy in a situation in which he believes that a stock's depressed price more fully reflects the negative news, only to see the stock continue to plummet. The trader has caught the proverbial falling knife.

# Wondering what it's like to work at a specific employer?

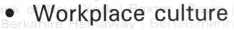

# Financial Products

## CHAPTER 5

Theoretically, a good trader should be able to trade anything and a good salesperson should be able to sell anything. Still, a lot of thought does go into the product you end up trading or selling. Wall Street is constantly dreaming up new products to meet the needs of its clients – this process eventually creates a need for these firms to support the active trading of these products in the secondary market. What follows is a brief description of the major product categories. This is not a comprenhensive list, but should give you a sense of the major product categories.

# Equity and Equity-Related Products

Equity markets provide a liquid market for the orderly trading of ownership interests (i.e., shares) in public companies. Shares are issued to investors who then have a stake in the company represented by a stock certificate. Listed or block trading involves all stocks traded on the New York Stock Exchange (NYSE), which prides itself on listing the biggest and best companies from around the world. The other major market for cash equities is the NASDAQ, which is home to both the best and the worst of the technology sector.

In addition to the different listing requirements of each exchange, there is also a fundamental structural difference between the NYSE and the NASDAQ.

## The New York Stock Exchange: the specialist system

Historically, equities have traded on the New York Stock Exchange (NYSE), the NASDAQ marketplace or the American Stock Exchange. The NYSE has typically attracted the largest "blue-chip" companies in America and has successfully expanded its listings to include such large foreign companies as Nokia and DaimlerChrysler. The NYSE is constantly rumored to be chasing after Microsoft (currently listed on NASDAQ) and has even reserved the ticker symbol "M" if Bill Gates ever has a change of heart.

In the NYSE, all orders are routed to the exchange floor. Floor brokers (also called "$2 brokers" because they used to charge $2 per trade) receive orders from traders working for investment banks and brokerage firms. Traders work on the desk and relay orders from salespeople and investors to the floor brokers or through a computerized order entry system (SuperDot, a small order executing system owned by the NYSE). Floor brokers represent buyers and sellers and gather near a specialist's post on the exchange floor to place buy and sell orders on behalf of their clients.

The specialist is the one professional responsible for a given stock (for example, IBM). He is responsible for matching up customer orders and providing liquidity when there is a buy or sell imbalance. These specialists work for NYSE specialist firms, who must have a seat on the exchange. The specialist is responsible for maintaining an orderly market in the security that he trades. Order is primarily achieved through the maintenance of an order book that indicates buy and sell orders at every market level. When stocks have a delayed opening, it is because there is a buy or sell imbalance, and the specialist will open the stock at the price where the most number of shares will transact. The NYSE argues that having one specialist maintains an orderly and fair market. Critics charge that the NYSE is a monopoly masquerading as a good corporate citizen.

The AMEX is a small-scale version of the NYSE. The AMEX has less stringent listing requirements and has recently gained prominence for its dominant market share in the QQQ, the NASDAQ 100 index trust that is the speculative vehicle of choice for the technology investor.

## The NASDAQ marketplace: Over-the-counter equities

The National Association of Securities Dealers Automated Quotation, commonly known as the NASDAQ, was created in 1971 as the world's first electronic stock market. The NASDAQ system is not an exchange – orders do not go through specialists. Instead, it is a decentralized screen-based system of interconnected terminals, through which dealers continuously update price quotations on approximately 5,x000 over-the-counter securities. Although the NYSE has the largest market capitalization of any stock market in the world, the NASDAQ actually is home to more issuers. Dealers are responsible for maintaining quotes in the box and must honor their display size. A quote for Microsoft might look something like this:

## Microsoft corporation:

| MLCO: | 23.05 – | 100 – 1 | GSCO: | 23.07 – | 1 – 199 |
|-------|---------|---------|-------|---------|---------|
| MSCO: | 23.05 – | 56 – 10 | ISLD: | 23.07 – | 5 – 150 |
| CSFB: | 23.03 – | 200 – 5 | PWJC: | 23.08 – | 10 – 20 |

The "inside quote" on Microsoft in this example is 23.05 – 23.07  100x199. Inside quotes are overall market quotes that represent the best bids and offers. In this case, Merrill Lynch is the best bid and Goldman is the best offer. The size of the market is 10,000 shares by 19,900 shares. If the bid is hit then MSCO stands ready to buy 5600 shares, and if Goldman is lifted, then Island has 15,000 shares for sale. Common misconduct that occurs is that the dealer "backs away" from his quote. In this example, Goldman is offered for 19,900 shares. Say you have 25,000 to buy for a client and you ask for 19,900, but the Goldman dealer only agrees to sell you 10,000 shares. Goldman makes the argument that a customer or a competitor was ahead, while you make the argument that Goldman isn't honoring his market and you call NASDAQ market regulation to settle the dispute.

# Risk Arbitrage ("merger arbitrage")

Risk arbitrage is focused on profiting from the eventual consummation of announced public mergers. The risk premium is defined as the spread that exists between the announced terms of the deal and the actual price at which the target firm is trading. Transactions with higher perceived deal risk (risk that the deal will not actually go through) trade with wider spreads (i.e., the risk premium) and less risky deals trade with tighter spreads. As the deal is ultimately consummated, this spread is eliminated and the risk arbitrage desk makes the difference.

### A risk arbitrage trade example

Disco Systems announces a deal to buy Southern Telecom. Disco agrees to exchange 1 of its shares for 2 shares of Southern Telecom. Following the announcement of this proposed transaction, Disco shares are trading at $20/share, and Southern Telecom is trading at $7/share. According to the terms of the transaction, Southern Telecom should trade at $10/share. If the deal is consummated as announced, the enterprising risk arbitrageur can make an expected profit of $6 by buying 2 shares of Southern Telecom and shorting 1 share of Disco. The risk arbitrageur is in the business of collecting these small risk premiums from numerous announced transactions. All else being equal, the risk arbitrageur makes money as the risk premium narrows over time. This expected narrowing of the spread does not always materialize. If the closing date of the deal is extended, then the spread widens to reflect the decreased probability of the deal closing successfully. If the deal is busted (i.e., target and acquirer fight or the Federal Trade Commission blocks the proposed deal), then the arbitrageur will normally get crushed. The goal of the risk arbitrageur is to collect more in risk premiums then he loses in occasional blow-ups.

# Fixed Income Securities

Governments, corporations, agencies, organizations, supra-nationals and financial institutions issue bonds to fund their activities. Bond market financing doesn't represent an ownership stake, but rather an IOU with interest. A few corporate bonds trade on the NYSE, but generally speaking, the fixed income market is an over-the-counter market. Within this vast over-the-counter market, screens and telephones facilitate trading activity. Institutional customers call dealers who trade order flow (dealers whose goal is to provide liquidity for customers rather than trade on proprietary accounts) based on the real-time information that is continuously updated on these broker-maintained screens. Phone-based OTC markets function through telephone calls. The institutional customer calls the broker-dealer who in turn calls brokers to see what type of inventory is available for sale or for purchase on the Street.

Fixed income instruments can be traded as either negotiable or non-negotiable. Non-negotiable loans are private transactions between two counterparties. Since these are private transactions, there's not much need for traders or salespeople to get involved, so just know that this market category exists. The other major market segment is comprised of negotiable debt instruments, which trade on secondary markets after they have been issued by the borrower. These instruments include bonds and notes, and structured securities such as asset-backed and mortgage-backed securities. Negotiable fixed income instruments also include a class of instruments called derivatives, which derive value from an underlying market variable such as LIBOR.

Another way of segmenting the bond market is to broadly divide the universe of fixed income products into two groups: government bonds and spread products. Government bonds are issued by the U.S. Treasury and are the risk-free standard backed by the full faith and credit of the United States government. Spread products are bonds issued by any other issuer-agencies, corporations, foreign governments and supra-national organizations. Spread products have additional default risk, and are quoted as a "spread over comparable Treasuries" that is, the difference in yield when compared to a treasury board of the same term. For example, if a 10-year U.S. Treasury bond offers a 3% yield and a 10-year IBM bond offers a 3.5% yield, the spread is 0.5%.

## Government bonds ("Govies")

U.S. Treasuries are the benchmark against which all other fixed income products are priced. If you enjoyed economics in college, this might be a great product area for you. Government bond desks are organized by maturity. "Treasury bills" are government bonds with a maturity of 1 year or less. The Treasury issues 3-month, 6-month and 1-year Treasury bills, which are discount securities that pay par at maturity. (The bills pay a set amount a bit above the original purchase price; this amount is called the par value of the security.) "Treasury notes" are securities that have a maturity exceeding 1 year but not exceeding 10 years. "Treasury bonds" (10- and 30-year bonds) are the longest-dated maturity instruments issued by the Treasury. Notes and bonds are both conventional semi-annual coupon-paying securities. Since October of 2001, the Treasury has suspended issuance of the 30-year "long" bond. The new long bond is the 10-year Treasury bond. The Treasury also issues STRIPS (Separate Trading of Registered Interest and Principal of Securities), or zero-coupon bonds. These securities allow investors to hold and to trade the individual interest and principal components of eligible Treasury notes and bonds as separate securities. A recent addition to the Treasury product are TIPS (Treasury Inflation Protected Securities) which pay interest based on the level of inflation.

The shortest maturity products are like trading with training wheels. It's tough to screw up if you're a 3-month bill trader or repo trader. (Repo and reverse repo are the business of borrowing and lending securities.) The seasoned veterans are on the long end of the curve, trading 10- and 30-year bonds – these instruments have the most price volatility for a given change in yield. Long-dated zero coupons are the most price volatile instruments in the government bond market, since the full value of the bond is received as a bullet at maturity.

While U.S. government bonds do not have any default risk, do not mistake this for meaning that bonds are risk-free investments. Even with the full faith and credit of the U.S. Treasury, govies are interest-rate sensitive, and the principal can fluctuate dramatically in different interest rate environments. However, for buy-and-hold investors, there is no interest rate risk, since the principal is fully returned at maturity.

## Agency bonds

Federal government agencies issue bonds to finance their activities. These agency bonds help support projects relevant to public policy, such as farming, small business, or loans to first-time home buyers. Agency bonds do not carry the full faith-and-credit guarantee of government-issued bonds, but they carry triple-A ratings due to the implicit guarantee that exists between the government and a government agency. This implicit guarantee allows the respective government agency to access low-cost capital to support objectives deemed to be consistent with the national interest. Federal agencies that issue bonds include:

- Federal National Mortgage Association (Fannie Mae)

- Federal Home Loan Mortgage Corporation (Freddie Mac)

- Farm Credit System Financial Assistance Corporation

- Federal Agricultural Mortgage Corporation (Farmer Mac)

- Federal Home Loan Banks

- Student Loan Marketing Association (Sallie Mae)

- College Construction Loan Insurance Association (Connie Lee)

- Small Business Administration (SBA)

- Tennessee Valley Authority (TVA)

## Corporate bonds

Corporate bonds are bonds issued by corporations to meet their short- and long-term working capital requirements. "Non-dollar corporate bonds" are issued in currencies other than the U.S. dollar. Secondary trading activities tend to be most robust at dealers that have strong deal flow and a reputable credit research department. These research departments are always analyzing prospective bond swaps and are searching for favorable relative value trades (e.g., swapping down in credit or within similarly rated paper for a pick-up in yield, or swapping up in credit for a minimal yield give-up).

Corporate bonds are typically divided into two markets: high grade and high yield. Whether a bond is high grade or high yield depends on credit ratings given to the company by credit rating agencies like Standard & Poor's and Moody's. The higher the credit rating, the lower the risk of default, and the lower the interest. High grade bonds are issued by companies with good credit ratings and offer a lower yield (interest) for investors. High yield bonds (also known as "junk bonds") are any issues that trade below BBB from Standard & Poor's and Baa from Moody's. Sometimes, in anticipation of a credit downgrade, high grade bonds can trade with spreads equivalent to high yield bonds and vice versa.

## International bonds

International bond markets are less regulated than domestic bond markets, and therefore carry greater default risk. Anytime an investor buys bonds outside of his local currency, he is also incurring foreign currency risk (the currency invested in can drop relative to the dollar), and in certain emerging markets, there is the added dimension of political risk (a coup will make bonds issued from that country lose their value really quickly). There are four main types of international bonds issued by corporations, governments, sovereigns and supranationals: foreign bonds, eurobonds, dragon bonds and gobal bonds.

1. Foreign bonds are issued by foreign borrowers in a domestic market denominated in that market's own currency. The domestic market authorities regulate the issuance of these bonds. An example of a foreign bond would be IBM (an American company) issuing bonds in the United Kingdom, or SAP (a German company) issuing bonds in the United States. Several of the largest foreign bond markets and their associated names are as shown in the chart below:

| COUNTRY OF ISSUE | MARKET NAME |
|---|---|
| United States | Yankee |
| United Kingdom | Bulldog |
| Japan | Samurai |
| Spain | Matador |
| Australia | Matildas |
| Portugal | Navigators |

Circling back to our two given examples, IBM issuing bonds in the United Kingdom would be a Bulldog issue, and SAP issuing bonds in the United States would be a Yankee issue.

2.  Eurobonds are instruments for unsecured debt issued by governments, banks, corporations and supranationals which are outside the domestic market of the currency of denomination. Eurobonds are sold to an international group of investors who are beneficial owners of the currency of issue but not resident in the country of that currency. This last attribute means that Eurobonds enjoy a less restrictive regulatory environment, since they are not subject to national laws or regulations. A further advantage of Eurobonds is that they can be issued in any country and in any currency other than that of its country of issue, affording maximum flexibility to the issuer.

The Eurobond market is a 24-hour over-the-counter telephone and screen-based market. The historical unofficial home of Eurobond trading is the United Kingdom.

3.  Dragon bonds are issued in any currency and trade on at least two of the "Dragon" exchanges – Hong Kong, Singapore or Taiwan.

4.  Global bonds are traded simultaneously in the Eurobond market and on one or more domestic markets. Global bond issuers are typically triple-A rated and are frequently accessing the capital markets.

# Elements of a Bond Trade: The Need for Anonymity

Cantor Fitzgerald is the dominant government bond broker, and it makes markets in all maturities for U.S. government bonds. Bond brokers act as intermediaries between dealers, between dealers and customers (e.g., Fidelity, Vanguard, etc.), as well as between customers. So why don't dealers sell directly to customers? And why don't customers trade directly with other customers?

The answer to the first question is that all else being equal, dealers would prefer to transact directly with customers (who potentially are less informed about the real value of a particular security). However, when a big firm like PIMCO is selling, there's probably not going to be anywhere else to offload the position except through the bond brokers. The second question is somewhat more nuanced. Customers might sell directly to other customers but for the problem that in so doing, PIMCO might be tipping its hand to the potential buyer, who becomes so spooked that PIMCO is selling that instead of buying decides to sit on the sidelines waiting for a more favorable supply/demand picture. Next to proper execution, the most important element that customers in fixed income (and really any market for that matter) demand is anonymity in the marketplace. This objective is best achieved through brokers who transact huge volumes on an agency basis and charge a commission. The convention in the bond market is that whoever hits the bid or takes the offer pays the commission, so the cat-and-mouse game that tends to evolve (among the broker-dealers at least) is who avoids paying commission on his trades.

### Calling in a bond trade

Most bonds and derivatives trade over-the-counter. To get a quote you need to call a broker-dealer. For example, Cigna may decide that it needs a quote on its bond portfolio. It can go to Bloomberg to get a rough idea of what its bond portfolio is worth. Bloomberg maintains an extensive and proprietary bond pricing database. But the reality is that fixed income traders scoff at the Bloomberg generic quote, and these quotes should be treated as a general indication of the bond's value rather than a real-time assessment. A more accurate quote can be achieved by faxing over the portfolio to a broker-dealer's fixed income bond trading desk. If it's just one bond, the trader at Cigna can call his sales contact at Merrill Lynch, for example, who will then ask for a quote from the appropriate trader. The trader will ask who the quote is for. He'll check what type of merchandise is for sale by the bond brokers and make a price, say "101 22 – 101 25, 5 million up." This means that the trader is willing to buy or sell 5 million bonds from Cigna at 101 22/32nds or sell 5 million bonds to Cigna at 101 25/32nds. This is a two-way market, and while the trader is definitely willing to buy or sell at the prices he's indicated, chances are good that the bid price is the one where he had to sharpen his pencil on, since he knows Cigna is an owner and is probably looking to sell some or all of its position. OTC trading relies on the relationship between the dealer and the customer. The customer who does not trust the first quote can make a few calls, but generally speaking he doesn't want to make too many calls, because by the time he's called Morgan Stanley and Goldman Sachs, the Street is getting worried that there's a seller in the market, and the bid will start to fade accordingly.

## Municipal bonds ("Munies")

Municipal bonds are issued by local and state governments. Typically, these securities are tax-exempt, and therefore trade at lower yields. Investors need to consider their individual tax brackets to consider the relative attractiveness of municipal bonds relative to comparable taxable bonds. Municipal bonds are favored by wealthy investors in higher tax brackets.

## Asset-backed securities

Asset-backed securities include any products that are secured by some type of asset. These products include securities collateralized by mortgages (mortgage backed securities), credit cards, aircraft loans, and so on.

## Mortgage securities

Mortgage securities represent an ownership interest in mortgage loans made by financial institutions to finance the borrower's purchase of a home or other real estate. Mortgage securities are created when these loans are pooled by issuers or servicers for sale to investors. A couple of types of mortgage securities that are worth knowing about:

### Pass-throughs or participation certificate (PC)

The issuer or servicer of pass-through securities collects the monthly mortgage payment from homeowners whose loans are in a given pool (a pool brings together loans of the same maturity and same coupon rate) and "passes through" the cash flow to investors in monthly payments. Most pass-through mortgage securities are issued by Ginnie Mae, Fannie Mae or Freddie Mac and carry an implied AAA credit rating. Most pass-through securities are backed by fixed-rate mortgages, but adjustable-rate mortgages (ARMs) are also pooled to create pass-through securities. ARMS typically have caps and floors. These option-like characteristics require a higher yield on the ARM-backed pass-through security.

### Real estate mortgage investment conduit (REMIC) / Collateralized mortgage obligation (CMO)

Mortgage-backed-securities collateralized by mortgage pass-through securities. REMICs allow cash flows to be directed so that different classes of securities with different maturities and coupons can be created.

## CMO Primer

Collateralized Mortgage Obligation (CMO) structures are complex. The following discussion is meant to give you a sense of whether or not this business is for you. If you don't particularly enjoy talking about TAC tranches and Z-bonds, then perhaps you should consider a less complex, more flow-oriented product.

The CMO is a multi-class bond backed by a pool of mortgage pass-throughs or mortgage loans. In structuring a CMO, an issuer distributes cash flow from the underlying collateral over a series of classes (called tranches). Taken together, these tranches comprise the CMO. CMOs have two or more tranches, and each tranche has an expected cash-flow pattern designed to meet the need of a particular investor. These expected cash flows are measured according to Weighted Average Maturity and Weighted Average Coupon. For example, a five-tranche CMO might have two-, five-, seven-, 10- and 20-year tranches. The actual realization of cash flows can be substantially different from the expectation if the assumed prepayment rate differs from the actual prepayment rate.

### Sequential-pay CMOs (plain vanilla CMO)

All scheduled and unscheduled principal payments pay down investors in the first tranches (alphabetically listed so that the A tranche is retired before the B tranche, the B tranche before the C tranche, and so on). Investors in later tranches have more prepayment stability than investors in earlier tranches, since the late tranches do not start receiving principal payments until prior tranchers are paid off.

### Z-bond (accretion bond)

Z-bonds are the final tranche of CMOs which do not pay interest ( this interest is accrued) until all prior tranches are retired. When the prior tranches are retired, the Z-bond receives coupon payments based on the higher principal balance and any principal prepayments from the underlying mortages. The Z-bond tranche helps stabilize the cash-flow patterns in the other tranches, but the Z-bond is itself a highly volatile debt instrument.

### Planned amortization class (PAC) and targeted amortization class (TAC)

The planned amortization class (PAC) and targeted amortization class (TAC) reduce investors' prepayment risk by establishing a sinking-fund structure. PAC and TAC bonds assure to varying degrees that their investors will receive payments over a predetermined time period under various prepayment scenarios. PAC bonds tend to provide more stable cash flow under a greater number of prepayment scenarios than TAC bonds.

To establish the desirable stability of PAC or TAC tranches, support or non-PAC bonds must be created to absorb the variability of collateral principal cash flows. Unscrupulous mortgage dealers often do not label these support bonds as such, but these support bonds will often be attractive to potential investors due to their higher yield.

### Floating-rate CMO tranche (Floaters)

Floaters pay a variable rate of interest normally tied to LIBOR. Variants of the floater include the superfloater (which pays a spread above LIBOR) and inverse floaters which vary inversely with LIBOR.

### Strips

Stripped mortgage securities can create bonds that receive some interest and some principal (strips). Mortgage securities that are completely stripped form interest-only securities (IO) and principal only (PO) securities. IOs and POs are more sensitive to changes in prepayment rates and interest rates than standard pass-through securities. POs increase in value as rates decrease, whereas IOs decrease in value as rates decrease. Think of a PO as a zero-coupon bond that has the additional risk of prepayment and is therefore less desirable than an option-free zero coupon bond in a falling rate environment (due to faster than expected prepayments) and also less desirable in a higher rate environment (again due to prepayments). Think of an IO as an annuity of variable maturity, which contracts in a falling rate environment and also receives less than expected interest payments. In a rising rate environment, the life of the IO extends, exactly at the worst possible time, when an investor would prefer to have as much income as possible to reinvest at higher rates. IOs are often used as hedges to fixed-income securities due to their unique return characteristics.

### Callable pass-throughs

The callable class receives all of the principal and interest from the underlying collateral. Rather than being short a series of call options to the underlying borrowers, the callable class investor is short a call option to another investor. The call class receives no principal or interest, but has the right to call the underlying pass-through from the callable class holders after a specified period of time has passed at a stated price. Consequently, the callable class receives a higher yield to compensate for more limited upside, relative to a straight pass-through.

# Convertible Securities

### Convertible bond basics

Convertibles combine the equity upside with the income characteristics of bonds. Convertible bond desks offer a nice work environment for people with an analytical bent who want something a little more exciting than bonds.

Here's a basic example of how a convertible bond might be structured: convertible bonds of Company X can be converted into 5 shares of Company X stock if its stock price rises above a pre-specified threshold. There are three determinants of value in a convertible bond: investment value, conversion value and option value. Investment value refers to the value of the convertible bond if it were a straight bond. This is the value below which a convertible can never trade. The conversion value is the value of the bond if it were to be converted into stock of Company X. In this case, if Company X stock currently trades at $20/share, and converting one bond for 5 bonds produces a conversion value of $100. If the conversion value exceeds the investment value, then conversion value takes precedence. Note that conversion value can only be positive since it is a right and not an obligation available to convertible bond investors. This option normally translates into a convertible bond price that exceeds the investment and conversion value. The present value of this premium represents the option value of the convert.

## Convertible arbitrage trade example

This transaction type consists of matching a long position in a convertible security (owning the security) with an offsetting short position (owning the right to sell at a certain price) in the underlying stock. The main driver of profitability in convertible arbitrage transactions is the current income generated by combining the yield of the convertible security with the interest income on the proceeds from the short positions, less any dividends on the shares sold short.

Additional profit is generated through delta hedging. First, the setup: suppose the price of a convertible bond is $1000, and that the company's current stock price is $75 with a 33% conversion premium, so the value of the stock conversion premium is $100. Option delta is the change in the price of the option for a 1% increase in the stock option. Assuming an option delta of 0.5, then the amount of shares to sell short is given by the following formula:

Hedge ratio = (Convertible bond price/Conversion premium) * Option delta
= ($1000/$100) * 0.5 = 5 shares

The hedge ratio indicates that for every 1 convertible bond owned, 5 shares should be sold short. For small changes in the price of the stock, this delta hedge creates a market-neutral position where the profit from this convertible arbitrage trade is the income from the short and the coupon on the bond. In volatile markets, this hedge breaks down and a large decrease in the value of the stock will create an additional profit, since the stock will lose more in value than the convertible. Similarly, if the price of the stock increases substantially, the convertible will gain more than the short stock position, again earning a profit for the convertible arbitrage trader. Typically, the bond side of the trade needs to be hedged, since if the yield curve shifts significantly, the trader could end up reaping an additional windfall gain or loss, which is not part of the game for most convertible arb trades.

# Derivatives

A derivative is an agreement between two parties in which each agrees to transfer an asset or amount of money on or before a specified future date at a specified price. A derivative's value is derived from one or more underlying variables. Originally, derivatives trading involved commodities as a way for farmers to hedge away the financial risk of their business, but today derivatives are tied to everything from currencies and interest rates to the weather.

A forward contract is a transaction in which the buyer and seller agree upon the delivery of a specified quality and quantity of asset at a specified future date. A price is normally specified in advance or at the time of delivery.

- A futures contract is a legally binding obligation for the holder of the contract to buy or sell a particular commodity at a specific price and location at a specific date in the future. The appeal of an exchange-traded future is that the contracts can be standardized, so that everyone in the market is trading the same contract.

- An option gives the buyer the right but not the obligation to buy (call) or sell (put) the underlying asset at a specified price (called the "strike price") up to or on a specific future date (expiration date). The buyer of the option pays the seller of the option a premium for this right.

- A swap is the simultaneous buying and selling of a similar asset or obligation of equivalent capital amount. This exchange of financial arrangements provides both parties with more favorable conditions than they would otherwise expect. For example, a payer of fixed-rate debt may desire paying floating-rate debt, and a payer of floating-rate debt may want to pay fixed-rate debt. If the two sides can agree on a notional amount upon which to compute coupon payments, then they can swap fixed for floating and floating for fixed. The notional amount never changes hands, and interest payments are netted.

### A look at swaps

How is a swap possible? How can both sides be made better off in an interest rate swap transaction? What we've learned from financial derivatives is that it's a tough world out there, and if you're making money, that's because you're breaking someone else's back (i.e., it's a zero sum game). If you've taken an international economics class, you may remember discussing gains from international trade. A similar concept is at work in the financial markets. Let's take a look at an example:

MMMM ("Four M") is a multinational corporation with a triple A credit rating. MMMM needs to borrow $100 million for 5 years. MMMM can borrow at a low fixed rate, but would prefer to take advantage of a floating rate basis loan.

Chewbacca is a triple B rated energy trading company named after the Star Wars character. Chewy needs to raise $100 million for 5 years. Because of Chewy's lower credit rating, it is easier for the firm to borrow on a floating-rate basis, or to issue debt with a high coupon. But alas, Chewy would prefer a fixed-rate loan in order to better predict future interest payments.

Each firm's situation is summarized below:

| RATES | MMMM CAN BORROW FIXED | CHEWY CAN BORROW FLOATING |
|---|---|---|
| FIXED | 6% | 10% |
| FLOATING | LIBOR | LIBOR + 1% |

Assuming that both corporations do not believe there to be substantial default risk, then an interest rate swap can be negotiated as follows:

1. MMMM borrows fixed rate at 6%

2. Chewy borrows floating at LIBOR + 1%

3. MMMM and Chewy enter into a $100 million notional interest rate swap agreement for five years such that:

MMMM makes floating rate payments of LIBOR + 1% to Chewy

Chewy makes fixed rate payments 9% to MMMM. Chewy agrees to make this higher fixed rate to MMMM because of its lower credit rating.

Now both sides of the swap look like this:

| | MMMM CAN BORROW FIXED | CHEWY CAN BORROW FLOATING |
|---|---|---|
| PAYS | LIBOR + 1% + 6% | 9% + LIBOR + 1% |
| RECEIVES | LIBOR | LIBOR + 1% |
| NET PAYMENTS | LIBOR – 2% | 9% |
| WITHOUT SWAP | LIBOR | 10% |
| SWAP SAVINGS | 2% | 1% |

Notice that the swap has allowed both MMMM and Chewy to achieve a lower cost of borrowing than either would have been able to access without each other. Notice also that these savings were possible even though MMMM had a lower fixed and floating rate available to it at the outset. These savings will be reduced by the dealer's fee for arranging the swap. In this happy world, customers and dealer both profit. Originally, dealers acted as matchmakers between counterparties. Today, the swaps market has become so standardized that dealers stand ready to take the other side of the proposed interest rate swap trade.

## Risk management

The main reason for using derivatives is to manage risk. The derivatives market offers hedgers like the CFO of a large industrial company a way to hedge away his firm's financial risk, and it provides speculators (who are hopelessly addicted to leverage) an opportunity to profit from a particular market view. Arbitrageurs keep the market efficient by exploiting any price discrepancies between different markets or between the derivative and the underlying asset. Derivatives can trade in three ways, explained in the following sections.

## Fixed income derivatives

Fixed income derivatives are any derivatives instruments which derive value from a fixed income security. Typically these instruments are structured by Wall Street firms as a way to reallocate risks from corporations (who are seeking to mitigate business or financial risk) to speculators (who are seeking risk exposure in the expectation of profiting from a particular market view). Dealers will create a derivative instrument, and to support the development of this market will subsequently engage in creating and maintaining an active secondary market. As the market becomes more developed, spreads that the dealers pocket decrease dramatically. When interest rate swaps were popularized by Bankers Trust, BT was able to extort exorbitant fees from relatively unsophisticated corporate treasurers. Today, the interest rate swaps market is a screen-based market with razor-thin margins, and credit derivatives are all the rage. One word of caution for the neophyte fixed income derivative enthusiast: Warren Buffet has characterized derivatives as "financial weapons of mass destruction." While Wall Street has peddled derivatives as an efficient manner of reallocating risk, as the Long Term Capital Management debacle demonstrated, there are tremendous amounts of counter-party risk, since risk ends up being concentrated in relatively few hands, and one default in the derivatives market can trigger multiple defaults throughout the system, threatening the integrity of the entire worldwide financial market.

## Equity derivatives

Equity derivatives trade listed and OTC equity options. OTC options are contracts structured by the firm to meet the needs of specific institutional customers. Listed options are exchange-listed products that are completely standardized and more liquid. Call holders have the right (but not the obligation) to purchase shares of the underlying company at a pre-specified price. Put holders have the right to sell shares of the underlying company at a pre-specified price. Dealers are typically sellers of options, and the vast majority of options expire worthless (out-of-the-money). Being short options is equivalent to being short volatility (some options desks now call themselves "Volatility Trading Desks"). Options give the right to buy or sell an underlying stock: the higher the volatility, the greater the price of the option; the lower the volatility, the lower the price of the option. When a desk is net short options, it is short volatility, and will profit if volatility does not exceed the implied volatility at which the options were sold at. Think of options desks as insurers who are constantly collecting small premiums, but must every once in a while make a large payout related to a natural or man-made disaster.

## Over-the-counter (OTC) derivatives

Dealers structure and trade just about anything that can generate a fee, but typically these structured products compete with standardized exchange-traded products. These products include currency and commodity derivatives, as well as interest rate swaps. Structured products like interest rate swaps will typically trade over-the-counter, whereas more standardized products are traded on exchanges such as the Chicago Board of Trade (CBOT) and the London International Financial Futures and Options Exchange (LIFFE).

By now you should understand that the OTC equity market, the OTC bond market and the OTC derivatives market are all inter-dealer markets connected by telephone and computer network. There is no centralized exchange floor.

---

# Trading Systems for Derivatives

### On the exchange floor (open outcry)

Note that structured products are normally built with standardized derivative securities, and that in most circumstances, the dealer must then go out and hedge the exposure that he's taken on from the client (at least until he can find another customer to take an equal and offsetting position) by going to the exchange. This requires the dealer to structure a hedge using standardized future and option contracts that trade on the exchange floors.

Regional exchanges are continuously rolling out new products to trade, and successful products tend to develop pockets of liquidity on one or two major exchanges. For example, the Philadelphia Stock Exchange has a booming business in currency options. The Chicago Mercantile Exchange trades, among other things, currency and equity options.

Some futures exchanges use specialists in the same way that the NYSE employs specialists as a buyer or seller of last resort. On other exchanges, like the NYME, a trade cannot be completed unless there is someone else willing to take the other side of the trade. The commodity futures prices are determined in an open and continuous auction on the floor by brokers acting as agent (preserving anonymity of the customer) or principal. This auction process involves a lot of yelling and hollering, and is appropriately called "open outcry." Highest bids are matched with lowest offers and supply and demand push the contract price in the appropriate direction.

---

### Electronic trading (GLOBEX)

Electronic trading was introduced as a way to extend the trading hours of the major exchanges, and today has grown into a big business. Electronic trading systems apply the same rules that are enforced on the trading floor. Customers enter bids and offers into the system. This information is disseminated electronically to all market participants, and the orders are matched off subject to the individual rules of the market.

# Trends in the Industry

## CHAPTER 6

## Technology Trends

A dominant trend affecting the equity, fixed income and derivative markets is the impact of technology on spreads. Information technology is constantly improving the efficient dissemination of information through the marketplace. This effect is mitigated by increased volume in trading (i.e., two nickels make one dime) but to the extent that this shortfall is not fully recovered, broker-dealers must accept lower commission income or seek to improve trading revenues by taking on more risk. The technology landscape is constantly changing and technologists envision a future trading landscape with no physical exchanges and a reduced role for market intermediaries. Of course, the NYSEs of the world don't see eye-to-eye with this vision of the future. And, while it's possible to automate the matching of customer orders, there is always a need for specialists and dealers to furnish capital when there is no liquidity in the marketplace. However, employing capital to trade with sophisticated investors is a riskier business than just trading order flow, and it is possible that the risk-adjusted return of trading desks will decline. Several constituencies that are exploiting technology to lower the cost of trading for buyers (at the expense of the established Wall Street dealer community) are worth keeping an eye on. Here's a look at some of them.

### Bloomberg trading

Bloomberg terminals, which deliver financial news information and data, have become ubiquitous fixtures on trading desks around the world. Bloomberg's trade book is an electronic crossing network (ECN) that seeks to leverage the installed base of terminals to generate trading revenues in the equity markets. Bloomberg's trade book is one of numerous competitors in the ECN that allow users to post bids and offers and to trade at a fraction of the cost charged by more established broker dealers.

### Cantor Fitzgerald/eSpeed

Cantor Fitzgerald created the world's first electronic marketplace ("screen brokerage") for U.S. government securities in 1972. eSpeed was introduced in 1996 as a fully electronic trading system that allows simultaneous electronic trading access to U.S. Treasury cash and futures markets.

## Broker-dealers

Broker-dealers are always banding together to respond to the latest threat posed by technology. There is very little innovation that actually goes on at broker-dealers (at least as it relates to new technology platforms), and the announced initiatives, for the most part, seem to be ineffective, since these initiatives are purely defensive in nature. For example, when Bloomberg first began to gain popularity, every major broker-dealer banded together to form the Electronic Joint Venture (EJV). This project failed miserably and Bloomberg has become the industry gold standard.

## NASDAQ

Having an information monopoly on NASDAQ pricing data isn't enough. NASDAQ is now getting into the stock trading game. The latest iteration of NASDAQ is called Supermontage and SuperSOES. According to NASDAQ, both initiatives attempt to improve transparency throughout the NASDAQ marketplace. Critics charge that these changes do nothing more than create a revenue stream for NASDAQ at the expense of the dealer community. You can read more about this or access NASDAQ market data on Nasdaqtrader.com.

## Reuters/Instinet/Island Securities

Instinet is an anonymous electronic trading platform for equities owned by Reuters. Since ECNs have proliferated, Instinet's profitability has been on the decline. The firm recently acquired the largest ECN, Island Securities. Instinet has typically been favored by dealers and institutions, while Island was the execution platform of choice for day traders. These two pools of liquidity are considerable, and are often taking the other side of each other's transactions. Now, Instinet controls both.

# Business Trends

There was a time when Wall Street was very focused on proprietary trading (trading with the firm's own capital with the goal of making a profit on very short-term incidents, as opposed to taking a cut for trading for a client) as a source of profit. John Merriwether's bond arbitrage group chronicled in Michael Lewis' *Liar's Poker* at Salomon Brothers was the perfect example. The problem is that proprietary trading profits are by their very nature non-recurring sources of revenue. A trader may make or lose a killing in Q1, but there's no guarantee that this profit opportunity will happen again in the future. Wall Street has increasingly backed off making big capital commitments to the proprietary trading effort, since they've discovered that investors don't pay a premium for a company with a volatile earnings stream.

However, sales and trading for clients in return for commissions, while not as profitable as investment banking, can contribute significantly to the firm's earnings. The tradeoff that has been made is that Wall Street has become increasingly customer-focused. The strategy here is that Wall Street firms already provide equity and fixed income research, as well as merger advisory and investment banking services to clients, so why not focus the firm's trading effort as a complement to the full range of services that the investment bank already provides? Customer-driven trading is very different from proprietary-driven trading, and its relative importance as a contributor to earnings has increased.

The bottom line here is that students who think that they're going to walk onto a trading desk and start buying shares of IBM for the firm's proprietary account will be disappointed. Traders don't care about where IBM shares trade – their sole function is to provide liquidity in the marketplace. This is a very challenging task, but it's a different game that's being played, and prospective job candidates need to be mindful of this shift.

# Education Trends

It used to be that the mail guy could get promoted all the way up to trader or head sales position. This is a story that a lot of current Wall Street veterans share, but it is increasingly becoming the exception rather than the rule. Wall Street's frenzy to hire from the best schools has extended to its sales and trading desks, and new analyst and associate classes are filled with recruits from Ivy League schools. Educational pedigree, even though it may have little bearing on whether or not the candidate will ultimately become successful, is becoming more important as a first screen into the business.

Consequently, it's becoming increasingly common for desks to recruit directly from the best Ivy League schools and a few other top schools. This is great news if you're at one of these schools, but otherwise it is not such a good thing. Each firm's commitment to hiring from this core group of schools is significant, but there are always ways around the system. Trying to develop contacts through your school's alumni network is probably the most effective way of landing a job on a desk if your're not at a targeted school.

But educational background doesn't just matter for getting a position – it also is important for ensuring a good "fit" in your position. For example, if you're the only MBA on the desk, you may end up getting a not-so-attractive nickname. If you have an MBA or an advanced degree, it may be easier for you to fit in by finding a department that has a number of advanced degree holders. Typically, since MBAs are always attracted to the latest and greatest in the industry, you'll find more MBAs populating sales and trading desks in hot product areas. You're more likely to find MBAs trading mortgage securities or fixed income derivatives rather than equities. Although it's certainly not a hard and fast rule, you're more likely to find an MBA-friendly work environment where there have been several MBAs that have paved the way ahead of you. If these former MBAs also happen to be alums from your school, then even better.

## A Note on Course Selection

If you're an MBA student, the electives you take can go a long way to helping you prepare for a career in sales and trading. The most important subject is economics. Macroeconomics gives you a broad exposure to the overall economy, and being familiar with what drives GDP and the trade deficit is very important, especially if you're considering a career in fixed income securities. Microeconomics is typically a prerequisite for MBA programs, and although it's interesting to learn, it's somewhat less useful than macroeconomics. Monetary economics is also extremely useful in helping to understand what levers the Federal Reserve has to stimulate or moderate economic growth.

Within the finance major, classes that teach you how to value financial instruments are highly recommended, especially if you're considering a career in options, derivatives and fixed income securities. Corporate finance gives you the basics of how to value a stock according to its free cash flows, but the reality is that equity salespeople and traders don't use discounted cash flows to value a prospective trade. On the other hand, options, derivatives and fixed income traders rely on their models to price securities – it is a more quantitatively challenging task, and taking classes like speculative markets and fixed income securities will definitely give you an advantage out of the gate. If your school offers a trading seminar, then definitely do everything you can to take the class. While not perfectly accurate, it gives you an opportunity to match wits with your classmates, and to make trading decisions in a fast-paced simulation exercise.

For undergrads, these higher-level finance courses are generally not available, but you can do your best to prepare by taking as many economics electives as possible. Engineering programs often have modeling courses that, while not directly applicable to finance, do teach a rigorous analytical framework which can be applied to the pricing of financial securities.

# ON THE JOB

# Career Paths and Employers

## CHAPTER 7

## Undergraduate Career Path

Wall Street recruits aggressively at the undergraduate level. Typically, most bulge bracket investment firms hire a significant portion of their summer interns for their full-time programs. The summer internship is typically a coveted position, but in reality there's not much a summer intern can do without being licensed (we'll discuss the Series 7 and 63 licensing exams in detail in the "Getting Hired" section). The glossy recruiting materials will tout a rotation through various product areas, classroom training and numerous social and professional schmoozing events. While these undoubtedly occur, the most significant tasks of the summer intern will include fetching coffee and ordering lunch. To the extent that trading can be learned by osmosis, the lucky intern has ample opportunity to monitor the stock market, watch the traders and maybe even listen in on sales calls to clients. All the phones on a trading desk have mute buttons, so interns and trainees can listen in on conversations with clients without being noticed. This last part is perhaps the most valuable aspect of the summer internship. In the end, however, the most important part of being a summer intern in institutional sales and trading is to be well liked, or at least not piss anyone off. It's very easy to make a bad first impression, and the trading desk can quickly become an extremely inhospitable environment for interns that don't fit in.

Full-time undergraduates are recruited into Wall Street analyst two-year programs. These programs are fairly standardized across the street. Most firms have a start date towards the end of July or early August. The entire class of S&T analysts first spends two to three months in New York City in a training program that serves as an introduction to the firm. Various managing directors and other officials within the firm will talk about their specific product areas (credit derivatives, corporate bonds, listed stocks, and so on). The training program will also include bond math and basic accounting – remedial for anyone that has a business background, but critically important for liberal arts and science majors for understanding the basics of the business.

At the end of the training program, the newly minted analyst will have to complete the Series 7 and Series 63 examinations with the NASD. Candidates interested in trading NASDAQ stocks will also have to complete the Series 55 examination. Typically, these exams are not very difficult to pass, but one should still take care not to fail the exam. Although not quite as embarrassing as failing the bar exam, new analysts should be wary of distinguishing themselves through failure. Concurrently or shortly after passing the industry licensing examinations, analysts will be placed into the various departments of the firm. The placement procedure varies by firm. Some firms hire directly for specific programs, and analysts know from the start which trading desk they will call home. Most firms, however, have a competitive placement process once analysts have been hired. Analysts will compete with other analysts for coveted positions on the desks with the most action. Whatever product area is hot is typically where most analysts and associates will want to be placed. This elaborate mating ritual is somewhat more forgiving than interviews, since in theory the analyst is supposed to rank his or her top three choices, and these choices are supposed to be considered when placement decisions are made. Miraculously, at the end of the day, most analysts are able to say that they ended up working for one of their top two choices.

## Analyst pay

As an analyst at a bulge bracket firm, you can expect starting salary between $45,000 and $55,000 and a year-end bonus of $20,000 to $30,000. Although this sounds like a lot of cash, remember that most sales and trading opportunities are in New York City, where $45,000 doesn't always get you very far.

On the plus side, you'll be making more than most of your classmates. Compared to your college roommate who's now an investment banking analyst, your per-hour compensation will work out to be substantially higher, although you're getting paid roughly the same dollar amount. In addition, there's a much better chance that an outstanding S&T analyst will receive an offer for continued employment at the firm at the end of the program. Investment banking analyst programs, by contrast, may offer the superstar analyst a third year, but after that, the analyst usually has to go to business school in order to move up.

Lastly, as an analyst, you won't see much variability in your bonus, especially if you're working in a large shop that has an entire analyst class. This can be a good thing if you're minimally incompetent, but not a very good thing if you're the next George Soros.

# The MBA in S&T

**Do I need an MBA to be promoted on a sales and trading desk?**

Generally, sales and trading is a much less hierarchical work environment than investment banking. For this reason, it is widely believed that you don't need an MBA to get promoted on sales and trading desks. This view is often perpetuated be people who work on trading desks, but just because you hear this once or twice, don't accept it as truth. Whether you need an MBA or not is really a function of the firm you work for and the desk you're on. If the firm you're considering hires both associates and analysts, but you notice that associates are offered twice as much pay as analysts, then this is certainly an indication that MBAs are more highly valued. This doesn't mean that you can't be promoted without an MBA; you'll just have to work much harder to get recognized. When it's time for a promotion, you may also be somewhat behind in the pecking order. Some firms, on the other hand, don't want MBAs. This may be because they don't want to pay more for employees with business degrees, or because they have an implicit firm policy regarding MBA – some firms hold the view that it's hard to teach an old dog new tricks, so they will hire exclusively out of undergraduate programs.

Not only is the MBA valued differently from firm to firm, but it is also valued differently from desk to desk. A lot about being on a trading desk is about fitting in, and if everyone else, including the boss, doesn't have an MBA, then chances are that having an MBA won't add too much value in this environment. In fact, an MBA degree may even hurt your career prospects if there's a downright disdain for MBA types. Alternatively, if the desk you're on is populated with MBAs, then not having an MBA will probably limit your career advancement. Alternatively, you can be in a situation where you're the only MBA and everyone thinks that you're the brain, which can work to your advantage even if the boss has no personal biases about the value of the degree.

The bottom line is that there are no hard and fast rules. Depending on the particular firm and desk, an MBA may not advance your career. Be aware of the aforementioned issues, and ask some good questions to get a better feel for whether an extra degree is a benefit.

**What are some of the tangible benefits of an MBA?**
The pay is better and you will generally have a faster track for promotion to salesperson or trader. The MBA associate will typically have to do the same demeaning things that an undergraduate analyst does, but mercifully for a shorter period of time. In some cases, MBAs are also more likely to be assigned the desk that they'd like to work for. Undergraduate sales and trading recruiting programs, on the other hand, may hire you as part of a generalist pool and place you on a desk that isn't your top choice. Another benefit for the MBA candidate is the availability of more exit options out of sales and trading.

# MBA Career Path

First-year MBA students and recent MBA graduates are eligible for summer associate and full-time associate positions respectively. Associates start with similar responsibilities as analysts, but add more responsibility quickly and are typically on a faster track for promotion.

MBAs are also more likely than analysts to have the opportunity to get staffed abroad. For example, Goldman Sachs, Morgan Stanley and Lehman Brothers have recently hired MBAs from American business schools directly into their European trading desks. MBAs interested in pursuing sales and trading opportunities abroad must be able to demonstrate local language proficiency, and a strong desire to make a long-term commitment to the region. Each of these firms has recently also offered summer internship opportunities, but these programs are less established than the New York-based opportunities, and therefore shouldn't be counted on as a stable source of MBA hiring demand.

## Associate pay: To infinity and beyond

Sales and trading associates will start at about the same base pay as their investment banking counterparts. As of 2004, the going rate at bulge bracket firms has held up around $80,000 to $85,000 per year plus a year-end bonus of $20,000 to $30,000. While signing bonuses were the norm during the bull market of the late 1990s, they are now rare. Salaries increase primarily through performance bonuses, especially if you've become a position trader for the firm. Bonuses are normally computed as a percentage of the trading revenues you generate (or commission dollars that you generate if you're a salesperson), so depending on how cheap or generous your firm is, this number can be normally expected to fluctuate between 0 percent and 10 percent in any given year.

If you make $10 million for the firm, however, don't expect to receive a cool million for your efforts. Wall Street firms are highly conscious of expense control, and the largest expense item is compensation. To keep compensation expense at or below 50 percent of revenues, investment banks hand out compensation packages that include among other things, cash, stock options and restricted stock (stock grants that vest over a period of several years). Generous stock option grants are a non-cash form of compensation that doesn't hit the income statement, but aren't quite as motivating as cash. Another game in the compensation is the granting of restricted stock. This is a major component of pay as you move up the ladder, and you can only convert this compensation into cash according to a vesting schedule that stretches out for years.

Finally, keep in mind that investment banks operate across all markets and products sectors. Full-service investment banks operate both a bond desk and an equity desk. The bond traders make more money and the salespeople sell more bonds when the economy is in recession. On the other hand, the stock traders make more money and the sales-traders sell more stock when the economy is robust. What happens at the end of the year when the compensation committee is determining how big the bond bonus pool and the equity bonus pool should be? Most firms tend to cross-subsidize the equity desk with the bond desk's revenues when the stock market falls on hard times, and to return the favor to the bond desk when the bond market falls on hard times. This makes sense at the corporate level (preventing mass defections, for example), but the immediate consequence to the stock trader who generated $10 million in revenues and is expecting a $1 million check is that he'll see a lot less than $1 million. The consolation to the expectant stock trader is that when he makes substantially less than his budget, maybe the bond desk will stuff his stocking.

## The winding promotion road in S&T

The path to promotion on a sales and trading desk is less standard than it is in investment banking. Investment banking analysts really don't have much too look forward to except perhaps a third year before shuffling back to business school or some other career. By contrast, undergraduate analysts who have a demonstrated ability to add value to a trading desk have the potential to move up without an MBA.

One common scenario is that after several years, the restless undergraduate analyst decides to apply to business school and gets accepted. If this analyst is a prized employee, then the boss might offer the analyst a promotion to associate in order to keep the analyst on the desk.

Title promotions on trading desks are generally not much to celebrate, except that they generally lead to higher pay. Whereas investment banking associates promoted from analyst can look forward to moving out of the analyst bullpen and into a real office with a secretary, S&T associates settle for better accounts and more trading responsibility. The focus of promotions isn't to achieve a particular title (vice president, director, managing director, etc.), but rather, to earn real sales and trading responsibility. Of course if you do your job well, you'll be duly compensated and promoted, but after reaching a level of significant responsibility, you shouldn't be expecting to getting a title promotion every couple of years.

# Experienced Candidates

There is no formal hiring process for experienced candidates. If you are in the position of trying to switch firms, then you better find a good headhunter. You cannot credibly hope to enter into the analyst/associate training programs since you have too much experience and are too expensive. A good headhunter can put you in touch with opportunities commensurate with your skill level and salary requirements.

## Switching desks

The good news here is that if you're a proven revenue generator and good at what you do, then chances are pretty good that you'll be able to find a new home somewhat more to your liking. Certain firms are more flexible than others – Goldman Sachs for example has a reputation for moving talented employees through different business units and divisions.

One reason firms are able to do this is that essential sales and trading skills can be applied to any product area. For example, an international equities trader going through a mid-life crisis might decide to try his hand at equity derivative sales. Alternatively, a government bond sales professional looking for a switch could consider any number of other fixed-income product areas, or maybe even equities. Within departments, it's especially common to switch sectors. For example, in the government bond market, you'll see that most traders start out in the Treasury bill market, and over time, if successful and willing, will move out on the maturity curve, eventually trading the long bond. Salespeople typically have pre-existing relationships with customers, but even while preserving these customer relationships, salespeople often work with different traders in different market conditions, giving the salesperson an opportunity to learn more about different market sectors. Sometimes salespeople who cover a particular package of accounts might switch over to a different product area entirely, while maintaining relationships with a key group of accounts.

## Becoming a manager

One of the ironies of Wall Street is that the best traders and salespeople eventually are considered for managerial positions – but the skillset that is required of managers is very different from what made them successful as producers. Still, the rationale of meritocracy dictates that successful managers must also have been successful traders or salespeople.

Managers are responsible for maintaining the profit and risk profile of the entire department. The best managers recognize their own strengths and weaknesses and trust their traders and salespeople to do what they do best. That said, the manager is almost always involved in large trade decisions. The manager must decide on the appropriate level of risk, the amount of capital commitment, and the value of the customer to the firm's current and future business.

# Top 10 Sales and Trading Firms on Wall Street

Not all trading desks are created equal. Firms have relative strengths and weaknesses, and what follows is a brief summary of the top 10 Wall Street broker-dealers and some of the traditional strengths that they are known for. This list is by no means comprehensive and should be considered only a starting point for investigation. Further information is available on the Vault web site and through each firm's corporate web site.

Because of the synergistic relationship between sales and trading (better traders induce more order flow and better salespeople generate more orders), each of the firms in the following staffs an A-list roster of traders as well as salespeople. When evaluating the best of the rest, the prospective job hunter needs to carefully consider firms that present themselves as having a strong sales department but a less capable trading department, and vice versa. It is rare for firms to come out and say that their sales department lacks certain capabilities, but a good tip-off is if a firm says it is "building up" its sales or trading capabilities. You should ask follow-up questions when a firm mentions this. Why is the sales or trading department less developed? Was there a recent mass-departure of salespeople or traders? If so, why did they leave? Does their departure impact the attractiveness of the opportunity presented?

Here's a look at the top sales and trading firms on Wall Street:

## Bear Stearns

Bear Stearns has traditionally been a bond powerhouse, especially in fixed income spread products. The firm has one of the most seasoned corporate bond desks, and regularly transacts over $500 million of bonds per day. Bear Stearns' fixed income expertise also includes mortgage-backed and asset-backed securities. Within equities, Bear Stearns is an active trader of OTC equities and has a top three market share ranking in more than half of the securities it trades. It also has a leading market share of secondary trading of structured convertible securities.

## Citigroup's Global Corporate and Investment Bank (formerly Salomon Smith Barney)

Citigroup has positioned itself as the "one-stop shop" leveraging research and underwriting capabilities to provide secondary market liquidity for its institutional investor. Its equity division employs over 900 professionals throughout cash trading, convertibles, program trading, equity derivatives and floor brokerage operations. Citigroup's acquisition of Salomon Brothers greatly enhanced Salomon Smith Barney's fixed income capabilities. Although Sandy Weil shut down the fabled Salomon Brothers bond arbitrage group, Citigroup is one of the world's leading market-makers of fixed income securities which include bonds, loans and derivatives.

## Credit Suisse First Boston

Like its competitors, CSFB maintains a broad range of activities in equities, fixed income and derivative products. CSFB maintains a top three market share position in U.S. and European equity trading. CSFB's fixed income franchise is organized by product and regional teams. Notable product groups within fixed income include corporate and credit products, and interest rate products.

## Deutsche Bank

Deutsche Bank has a strong franchise in Europe and has been expanding its U.S. operations even as other European competitors have abandoned their U.S. growth aspirations. Deutsche Bank has supported its expansion through acquisition by acquiring BT Alex Brown (Deutsche Bank's OTC equity trading desk is located in Maryland where Alex Brown was headuartered). Deutsche Bank offers a full range of equity, fixed income and derivative capabilities, but generally is only recognized for excellence in German and European industry award categories.

## Goldman Sachs

The Goldman Sachs equities division is ubiquitous throughout global equity markets. It has access to the top issuers and institutional clients, and this translates into a very profitable equity business in equity market making and block trading. Not to be outdone, Goldman's fixed income, currency and commodities division (FICC) is at the forefront of worldwide markets in interest rate securities, foreign exchange, commodities and the evolving credit businesses.

## J.P. Morgan Chase

J.P. Morgan has a prestigious name brand that's recognized throughout the world, but J.P. Morgan's strength in sales and trading has traditionally been limited to products that are capital intensive. While J.P. Morgan maintains global equity, fixed income and derivative capabilities, its franchise is strongest in structured finance obligations, interest and credit derivatives, senior debt and loan trading.

## Lehman Brothers

Lehman Brothers is one of the world's top bond-trading firms and is a leading global market maker in U.S., European and Asian government bonds, money market securities, corporate bonds, mortgage and asset-backed securities, preferred stock, municipal bonds, bank loans and currency and derivative securities. This franchise is supported by the Lehman Brothers Bond Indices, which are the benchmark by which institutional bond portfolios are measured. Lehman Brothers is also a leader in U.S. and pan-European listed and over-the-counter stock trading.

## Merrill Lynch

Merrill Lynch has a long tradition of innovation in equity derivatives, creating the ever popular Liquid Yield Option Note (LYON) and the more recent tax-efficient iteration of this product. Merrill Lynch is a top trader of global equities. It has been the top trader of listed stocks since 1989, and the top trader of American Depository Receipts (ADR) since 1997. The firm also maintains a substantial NASDAQ/OTC operation. Merrill's global debt markets sells, trades and structures fixed income and derivative securities out of 17 countries for its institutional clients.

## Morgan Stanley

Morgan Stanley maintains a major presence in every major equity, fixed income and derivative securities market throughout the world. The fixed income division consists of three major global product areas: credit product group, interest rate and currency products and commodity products. The institutional equity division consists of the following global product areas: listed, OTC, international, research sales, convertibles, financial strategies group, listed derivatives and program trading. Morgan Stanley also produces and maintains the MSCI indices, which are the most widely used performance benchmarks in the fund management industry.

## UBS

UBS operates the world's largest trading floor in Stamford, CT. UBS is widely recognized as a market leader in eurobonds and is expanding its presence in global bonds. It is also a major force in foreign currency trading. Through the firm's integration of Paine Webber, the firm has enhanced its mortgage and asset-backed securities business. The acquisition of Enron's energy-trading book has established UBS in the energy trading business. UBS is also a leading bank in foreign exchange and treasury-related products.

### Best of the rest

Other bulge-bracket firms that attract talent for their sales and trading desks include: A.G. Edwards & Sons, Banc of America Securities, Prudential Securities, SunTrust Capital Markets, Wachovia Securities, Cantor Fitzgerald, William Blair & Co. and U.S. Bancorp Piper Jaffray.

Many other smaller firms maintain trading desks in numerous different product areas. These internships or full-time opportunities are somewhat more difficult to find, since these firms will tend to have less visibility on their hiring needs, and they typically chose not to incur the cost of doing on-campus interviews.

# Boutiques, Regional Firms, Foreign Firms and Specialists

### Boutique and specialty firms

Boutique firms tend to service one type of customer very well, or are very good at one type of transaction. Specialty firms focus their expertise on covering one or several market sectors, and can be thought of as mini-investment banks with a sales desk to support the trading effort, and investment bankers trying to nab the big deal away from the larger firms on the basis that the firm offers specialized service and expertise in a particular market niche. Boutiques and specialty firms include: Kaufman Brothers, Laqdenburg Thalmann, Arnhold S. Bleichroeder, Neuberger Berman, Fulcrum Global Partners, Miller Tabak & Co, Sanders Morris Harris, Sanford C. Bernstein, Fox-Pitt Kelton, Soundview Technology, Jefferies & Co., Thomas Weisel Partners, Weeden & Co., S.G. Cowen & Co., C.E. Unterberg Towbin, Robert W. Baird and Gerard Klauer Mattison.

## Regional firms

Some firms swim in small ponds and pick up the business that the NYC junkyard dogs overlook. These firms can be good alternatives for those who either are unable to land a position at a bulge-bracket firm initially, or who wish to live outside New York City. In some cases, specialty regional firms focus on one sector of the market that happens to be geographically concentrated in one region. Regional firms include: Adams Harkness & Hill, Allen & Company, Oscar Gruss & Son, Miller Johnson Steichen Kinnard, Johnson Rice & Co, Janney Montgomery Scott, MHMC Meyerson & Co., Ferris Baker Watts, Wedbush Morgan Securities, RBC Dain Rauscher, Legg Mason Wood Walker, McDonald & Co., First Albany, Pacific Growth Equities, J.B. Oxford & Co. and Friedman Billings Ramsey.

## Foreign firms

Foreign banks are always trying to establish a foothold in the U.S. market, and fail with alarming frequency. Here are several firms to consider: Credit Lyonnais, BMO Nesbitt Burns, CIBC World Markets, Scotia Capital Markets, TD Securities, Nomura Securities, Daiwa Securities and Dresdner Kleinwort Wasserstein Securities.

## Options-related firms

These are typically floor-trading positions on regional or secondary exchanges. Options trading is a very entrepreneurial business – all it takes is a seat on the exchange, a willing trader and a financial sponsor. The more developed a firm becomes, the more it is able to invest in a sales organization to solicit order flow. Even with a sales organization behind you, life on an options exchange is typically nasty, brutish and short. Traders on certain regional exchanges frequently brawl for customer orders, so it doesn't hurt if you've ever been in a rugby scrum before. Firms in this category include: Susquehanna Investment Group, O'Connor & Co., OTAA, Timber Hill, Van Der Moolen Options U.S.A., SLK-Hull Derivatives LLC, Knight Financial Products LLC, Group One Trading, GPZ Trading, Botta Capital Management and GVR Company.

## Specialist firms

Two decades ago there were more than 50 specialist firms. Since then, these predominately family-owned businesses have merged or been acquired. Today, there are only 10 specialist firms, three of which specialize in exchange-traded funds. Each firm is responsible for the orderly trading in the stocks that it is assigned. In the past, specialists earned their keep by charging a commission for matching up buyers and sellers. As spreads have narrowed with decimalization, specialists have relied increasingly upon principal trading – buying and selling for their own account. Specialists basically stand at their post and wait for orders to come in. There is not much need here for a sales organization, since once a stock has been assigned to a specialist, there's no way a stock that's traded by the firm can trade away from the firm-staffed post in a particular security.

Of course, when a new stock becomes listed through an IPO, specialist firms actively seek to be named as the firm that will cover the new issue. Needless to say, the NYSE's decision on who gets to be the specialist for the stock can get quite political. The seven stock specialist firms are: LaBranche & Co., Spear Leeds & Kellogg Specialists (owned by Goldman Sachs), Fleet Specialist, Van Der Moolen Specialists USA, Bear Wagner Specialists, Performance Specialist Group, and Susquehanna Specialists. The first five firms on this list trade over 95 percent of the NYSE's share volume.

The remaining three specialist firms, Bear Hunter Structured Products, SLK Index Specialists and Susquehanna Index Specialists are responsible for the orderly trading of exchange-traded funds (ETFs).

## Wholesalers

These firms are low-cost traders of large volumes of OTC securities. Wholesalers are, as their name implies, firms that specialize in trading OTC equities at low cost. These firms typically have a sales organization to support the firm's traders, but there is not much of a commitment to investment banking relationships. These firms make their profits by trading large volumes to make up for the lower commissions. Wholesalers include: Bernard L. Madoff Securities, Knight Securities, Charles Schwab & Co., Pershing (owned by CSFB), National Discount Brokers (Sherwood Securities) and Herzog Heine Gedould (owned by Merrill Lynch).

## Use the Rankings

A valuable resource for researching employers is the annual industry rankings compiled by a number of industry publications. *Institutional Investor*'s "II rankings" are the most well known, but other respected publications with rankings include *Global Finance*, *Global Investor*, *International Financing Review*, *Asiamoney*, *Euromoney*, *Risk* and *AsiaRisk*. When analyzing these rankings, there are several factors to consider. First, you want to see how the particular bank that you're interested in ranks in the product area that you are most interested in. Consistently high rankings over a number of years (i.e., not just a one-year wonder) should also be considered positive. Typically these rankings are derived through extensive client polling. Beware of firms' trumpeting of any individual ranking. These rankings are sliced and diced innumerable ways – three months vs. six months; announced mergers vs. completed mergers, and so on. So any one ranking isn't your best guide to who's tops in the field; the aggregate picture when looking at many rankings is a much more solid comparative study.

Be careful to note when the survey was performed and be sure to keep current on the latest news within the industry. If Merrill's listed trading desk won top honors for 10 consecutive years but then the Managing Director and a group of traders left Merrill for Morgan Stanley, chances are good that Merrill's ranking will drop the next time the survey is conducted. Also, be sure to note how a firm's overall research effort is ranked. Although the research department is often referred to derisively as a "cost center," when all other things are equal, a strong research effort is accretive to the overall sales and trading effort. A well-established research department leads to more commission dollars and investment banking revenue which increases the firm's visibility and prestige in the marketplace. In this hyper-competitive business, the importance of analyst coverage and name-brand research analysts cannot be overstated.

If a firm you are interested in is conspicuously absent from the rankings for the product area you are interested in, you might want to ask your contacts or interviewers there why. The most common answer is that the firm is building up its capabilities in that particular product area. This is especially true of European investment banks that have always coveted the U.S. markets but have made very little progress. But you should probe further. Is the firm leveraging a core strength? Is the management fully committed to riding out the ups and the downs of the market cycle to build this business? What is the background of the managers of this desk?

As an analyst or as an associate, you want to know that if you're not playing for the Yankees, you are at least playing for a team that is striving for greatness. As an analyst you want satisfactory answers to these questions. As an associate, these questions are even more important, since your promotion and future success depend on a stable organization with decent growth potential.

# Lifestyle and Workplace Diversity

## Lifestyle

Salespeople and traders revel in the lifestyle afforded by their jobs. They love the fact that they're done when the market closes. And it only gets better: generally speaking, the more senior a trader is, the sooner he or she gets out after the market closes.

The one negative to working market hours is that you've got to get up very early to get to work. Typical fixed income and equity desks are fully staffed by 7:30 a.m. For most people, this means getting up at least one hour before that. International equity traders who are trading London hours are in even earlier. Investment bankers, by contrast, begin rolling in the door after 9:00 a.m.

In contrast to most investment bankers, S&T professionals actually get to take their vacations. When senior traders are out, junior traders have an opportunity to step up. Normally there's a pecking order among the junior trading staff. The worst way to lose your position on this list is to trade the pad and lose a ton of money. While this is not a regular occurrence, it is very unpleasant and junior traders who step into this responsibility when a senior trader is on vacation need to strike the right balance between being aggressive and being cautious with someone else's P&L. Junior salespeople have a tougher time earning this type of backup role. Most of the time, if a salesperson is out on vacation, it's easy enough to re-assign that person's accounts to the remaining sales staff. This minimizes any disruptions to the level of service to the client, but it also doesn't provide a learning opportunity for junior salespeople. When a junior salesperson develops the confidence of management, that salesperson will be given an opportunity to develop his own book of business, typically starting with accounts that have not done very much business with the firm in the past.

Lunch is also worth talking about. There is a rather unpleasant hierarchy whereby summer interns and first-year analysts and associates are expected to fetch coffee and take lunch orders. Junior staff on trading desks have been known to trek to Hoboken for special-ordered sandwiches for the Jersey mob, or to Brooklyn for steak and shrimp cocktails. But just because taking lunch or coffee orders doesn't seem important, doesn't meant that it isn't. If Joe orders a medium coffee with cream, don't give him a Frapuccino. The more you screw up, the more often you'll be sent on coffee runs. The logic here is, if the kid can't even take a coffee order, what reason do we have to think that he can take a stock order? This is a rite of passage – almost everyone has experienced it, and there's no way around it.

Senior traders leave around 4:01 p.m. Analysts and associates at this point begin cleaning up the traders' mess. This means going through the trade blotter, matching up trades, confirming prices and knowing trades with other dealers (settling the trades at the end of the day). Woe to any analyst who has not paid attention during the day to keep a running tally of what his trader has done for the day. Some traders have typical type A personalities – they remember every detail of every trade, and are not impressed when the newly minted Ivy League grad can't keep up. On the other hand, some traders can't even remember what they had for breakfast – in this case, the analyst needs to protect the trader from himself. In either circumstance, it is advisable to note the details of every trade in the system and make sure you know exactly what happened. The best time to do this is right after the trade is done – it's fresh in everyone's mind and there's less possibility for error.

## Desk or Floor?

Working on a trading desk (e.g., trading foreign currency options on the trading desk) and working on the floor (e.g.., working on the Chicago Mercantile Exchange Floor) are two completely different experiences. Working on the desk is more comfortable – you can sit at a desk instead of stand in a crowd. Whenever a big economic number is about to be released, CNBC will normally do an interview with a local trader on the Chicago Board of Trade. That colorful mass of humanity in the background is the trading floor, and to survive, you need to be loud and aggressive. There are also hand signals that you need to learn.

Floor traders will argue that being on the floor gives them unique insight into the flow of the business. You get to see the raw human emotions of the business, you are competing with the best to make the right price on every piece of business, and you get a more complete picture of supply and demand dynamics of the business. The downside is that life on the floor can be quite unpleasant – people can be nasty and rude to each other. Because of this, floor traders have a high burnout rate. Generally, specialist firms have floor traders and "upstairs" desk traders who work together as a team. The upstairs traders structure trades and the floor traders execute the components of these trades. Both the upstairs traders and the floor traders will trade opportunistically for the firm's account.

## Q&A with a former (successful) floor trader:

**What did you trade?**
I traded Options on Futures of all the major USD vs. G-7 currency pairs (ie USD/JPY, EUR/USD, GBP/USD, USD/CHF, USD/DEM, USD/CAD) at the CME and PHLX

**What's the main difference between a floor trader and a desk trader?**
It really depends on what type of trader you are talking about (i.e., equity vs. bonds, prop vs. market maker). In my case I was making markets on Fx options. The biggest difference was centralization. On the floor you have access to all the traders in one central pit – this allows for a fast execution as you can trade with several people very quickly. OTC you have to call each individual bank or broker in order to get a price. Realize this is only for the options, a lot of OTC spot is done electronically and even the OTC options have moved this way recently. On the floor, 90 percent of the traders are locals working for themselves or a small partnership or company. These guys have a limited amount of capital and are often unable to take down big size. The other big difference is the physical aspect – on the desk you get to sit in a comfy chair all day and eat at your desk – on the floor you have to stand shoulder to shoulder and there's no eating or drinking allowed. Also, collusion is a lot easier on the floor.

**What type of coordination is there between the floor and the desk?**
At a bank that has both floor and OTC operations traders often share price and flow information and might leg into an arbitrage if the markets are different. The arb is very popular in the S&P's. There are guys that just trade the S&P futures against the basket of stocks in order to pocket the difference.

**What did you learn in school that made you a better trader?**
The best thing I learned at school is how to compete. (I think, due to the grade structure, this is severely lacking at the MBA level.) Futures

and options trading is a zero sum game; being smarter than the other guy and taking the right side is very important. There are winners and there must be losers. A desire to be the best and be a winner at school translates into good trading on the job. Also, school gave me a good work ethic that is important in trading. People who work hard at school will do so at trading and this usually pays off. In terms of specific classes, I think statistics is very important. Understanding how prices are distributed with help you understand the length and range of different security moves. Also, any class with game theory that helps you think strategically.

**What did you enjoy most and least about floor trading?**
The most: the learning experience. It is much easier to learn how to trade on the floor than a desk because you can see and hear the greed and fear in traders eyes and voices. The least: standing up all day, which really hurts your legs and feet. Also, it is generally a dirty place – the physical location, the people, the conversation...

**What advice do you have for aspiring floor traders?**
Use the floor as a learning experience then get out. Electronic trading is the future and where you want to be. The ISE – International Securities Exchange – is now the second most popular equity options exchange after having been around for only a few years. The specialist system is the only thing saving the NYSE – it provides a more orderly market.

# Diversity

An important aspect of sales and trading is that it is predominately white and male. Although no one on the inside will admit it (especially to anyone on the outside), there is still a great deal of gender and ethnic-bias built into the sales and trading culture. This is most apparent in the types of jokes that are circulated from one desk to another. If this is not an environment that you are comfortable with, then take this as fair warning. If you're passionate about sales or trading, but are uncomfortable with this type of environment, then it makes sense for you to try and visit the desk before making any decision on an offer.

# Q&As with Women S&T Professionals

To give you a sense of what it's like to work on a trading desk as a woman or minority, we've interviewed several people in this position.

### Fixed Income Salesperson

**Q. What do you trade/sell?**
I work on the fixed income side, focusing on corporate bonds and credit derivatives.

**Q. How did you get interested in sales and trading?**
I was interested in working for an investment bank. As a career switcher, I diligently attended all the company presentations on campus, and quickly settled on sales and trading. My prior position was in hospital sales. I used to be on the phone all day long selling, and I figured that selling on Wall Street can't be too much different.

**Q. I noticed that the only woman in the Boiler Room was the secretary. Obviously real life is different. How is it like working as a woman in the super-macho sales and trading environment?**
It's not easy. There are very few female MDs or VPs on the business side. Most women are either sales or trading assistants, with a slight bias for women in sales. Perhaps this is the face of the future, or perhaps it's the glass ceiling. Successful women in this business work hard. A saleswoman that I work with has been in the business for over 20 years. She graduated from Wharton and has a reputation for making a lot of money and for being a workhorse – she competes with the best salesmen on the desk on a regular basis. Of course she rarely goes out drinking with the boys, since she has to go home to her kids. Another factor here is that a lot of women have husbands of means and often end up quitting the business to take care of the kids.

**Q. Do you find the jokes on the trading desk to be offensive? How do you handle this?**
It's hard to ignore everything, but I do my best to ignore the really tasteless stuff. Although the trading desk is definitely raucous, at the end of the day, most guys realize that this is a place of business, and they will conduct themselves accordingly. Going for drinks after work, however, can be a totally different experience.

**Q. How do you manage the work/life balance? How have you observed others managing this balance?**

The really successful people in this business (men or women) spend a lot of time working at the job. There's really no way around it. To be successful you have to be a little obsessive about your career.

**Q. Do you feel that your quality of life is higher than your friends' in other industries?**
Great question. The answer is that it depends on your definition of quality of life. If your definition of quality of life means the person with the most money, then the answer is maybe. Sales and trading involves getting up at ridiculously early hours and going to bed before the 10 o'clock news. There's always the image of a trader holding a losing position and having a heart attack on the floor. While this undoubtedly happens, stress in this business is more insidious. It's monotony interspersed with stressful situations day after day after day. Most people in this business are young and physically fit, but it's incredible how many people have ulcers or high blood pressure. That's not to say that this business isn't for the right person. What I would say is that you need to have more of a reason to get into sales and trading than wanting to score the fast buck or not wanting to work in the investment banking sweatshop. One of the MDs I work with has been around since before the 1987 stock market crash. He still gets up at 4:30 a.m. every morning and is the first one to log onto the Bloooberg to check the news. This isn't because he has to – it's because he loves the business.

## Mortgage-backed Securities Salesperson

**Q. What do you trade/sell?**
Mortgage-backed sales – this includes just about anything that is securitized, from commerical MBS, asset backeds, CDOs. Although they are not my primary focus, I do end up selling some Treasury, Agency and derivative products as well.

**Q. How did you get interested in sales and trading?**
Although it may sound kind of corny, I really have always been somewhat interested in the markets because my father was in the business for 35 years, albeit on the equity side.

**Q. I noticed that the only woman in the Boiler Room was the secretary. Obviously real life is different. How is it like working as a woman in the super-macho sales and trading environment?**
What they say is true – you indeed MUST have a thick skin (although I would say this goes for pretty much anyone who is entering the trading environment from a different business or directly out of college). I usually just remind myself that if someone is yelling (at me or otherwise)

it probably has little to nothing to do with me (or the individual in question). My desk has really come a long way in the last few years – publicly chastising or berating someone is much less tolerated. With regard to being one of the few women in fixed income, my firm is a very family-oriented place and with few exceptions, most of my male colleagues are not pigs. Don't get me wrong, there are times I shrug and roll my eyes at some of the things I hear people say. Quite honestly, though, people on the Street want to make money and if you can contribute to the bottom line, you will be accepted. I would add that it helps if you like sports and play golf because it gives you something additional to discuss with your male colleagues. On a related note, most of my customers are male and dealing with them at times can be trickier than dealing with my colleagues on the desk. I have had a few men say inappropriate things to me but I really just do my best to shrug it off and move on.

**Q. Do you find the jokes on the trading desk to be offensive? How do you handle this?**

At times I am offended but I really believe that these jokes are told in all workplaces, not just on a trading desk. The difference is that everything we do and say is out in the open so it is challenging to close your eyes/ears to lewdness. I am not a shy person so will definitely open my mouth if I find something offensive. The best way to get someone to realize that what they are saying is inappropriate is to make them self-conscious.

**Q. How do you deal with uncomfortable situations that may arise when you go out with the guys after work?**

Again, I have to first say that most of the guys I work with are genuinely nice, fun people who are married or involved in serious relationships so they behave themselves. I think I distance myself a bit from the few pigs I know on my desk and thus have not had to deal with anything too bad. I have had to 'chaperone' some of the younger girls on the desk when they have gone out with a specific individual because I did not trust him to not try to exert his seniority over them. Also, since I am pretty forthcoming and outspoken, I am quite adept at avoiding touchy situations. Finally, I have spent most of my adult life working in male-dominated industries (after attending Dartmouth as an undergrad) I am kind of used to it!

**Q. How do you manage the work/life balance? How have you observed others managing this balance?**

It is not always easy but as I indicated earlier, my firm is a family-oriented place. For example, a woman with a toddler recently started working from home two days a week and it seems to be going well thus far. That being said, it seems like after a second or third child, more women opt to stay home. I am frustrated at times by the flippant male who will proclaim how easy it is to have a family and work. Of course it is for them when they have a stay-at-home wife and a nanny!

**Q. Do you feel that your quality of life is higher than your friends' in other industries?**

Yes. Although at times I wish I had an office and could close the door, I thrive in my work environment. I don't work late at night (other than entertaining) and have my weekends free 99 percent of the time. I do get to work very early in the morning (before 7) but I am used to it. For the most part we are very well paid especially considering how much fun we have.

# GETTING HIRED

# The Hiring Process

## Hiring Process

The front-door hiring process for analyst/associate programs is on-campus recruiting, which for most campuses and firms takes place in October and November. Most investment banks conduct on-campus interviews at their target schools for their sales and trading analyst and associate programs. Students who do well are invited for a second (and generally final) round of interviews at the firm's headquarters.

In addition to the typical behavioral interview, you should also be prepared for the "stressful" interview – an interview in which the interviewer is very confrontational or disagrees with what you're saying just for the sake of disagreeing. This is a modified behavioral interview meant to separate out the cool and composed candidates from the ones whose nerves fray easily. The rationale here is that if you fall apart during the interview, chances are good that you'll do the same on the desk – you're deemed to be an undesirable candidate.

Students attending non-targeted schools should forward resumes directly to the human resources departments of banks. Know that to be considered with the associate/analyst candidate pool, you may have to be willing to wait until the next incoming analyst class is fully assembled unless you start extremely early in the school year. It is very rare that banks will hire you even in December for the class whose training program begins in July.

The back door into the business is through connections. Some firms, notably Bear Stearns, have a very strict "no nepotism" policy, but this shouldn't discourage you from picking up the phone and calling a friend or friend of a friend on a desk. You may be able to meet someone and get an interview. Generally, though, this avenue only works for lateral hires moving from another firm, not entry-level hires graduating from school. Whether you're an entry-level or lateral candidate, if you're networking for a sales and trading job, be mindful of the fact that you are asking for a favor. For example, don't call your contact at 9:29 a.m. or 3:45 p.m. if you're thinking of an equity position – calling when the market is opening or closing is sure to create an extremely poor first impression. E-mail is a better, less-intrusive way of getting someone's attention – if the contact is interested in having a conversation, an appointment can be set up over e-mail.

## Resumes and cover letters

Cover letters and resumes should be sent directly to the sales and trading recruiter of the bank. Resumes should be limited to one page, and cover letters should also be brief. The standard advice for resumes applies: address the letter to a specific person rather than the "Human Resources Department."

For candidates with no prior industry experience, highlight any stock market experience that you have had. If you've managed a personal portfolio, be sure to mention this on your resume. In your prior work experience, be sure to highlight significant team responsibilities that you have had.

# Internships

As with any industry, an internship is the best way to determine whether or not this profession best matches your skills, abilities and interests. It also gives employers a relatively low-cost way to try potential employees out, after which they can hire interns they feel will fit well in their organizations.

The best place to start an internship search is your school's career placement office. Every school does it a little differently, but usually, there is a treasure trove of information available at the office. You can use this information to supplement information that you can get from your target firms corporate web sites. Be sure to seek out other students who have worked at your target firm to get their perspective on the firm's culture and what type of summer or full-time experience they had.

On-campus first-round interviews for internships are generally held in January and February. The hiring process for summer internships is the same as that for full-time analyst/associate positions (one round on-campus than another at the firm's office).

Generally speaking, the pay you can expect for the summer will be the typical analyst or associate salary prorated over the 10-week summer period. Do not expect any performance bonus or sign-on bonus as part of your summer compensation package.

## Should I cold call the desk to get a job?

Breaking into the institutional sales and trading industry is very difficult. Cold-calling, generally, is difficult, and while you certainly can get a job this way, be prepared for rejection. The industry has built up substantial human resource infrastructures that are tremendously valuable in the formalized job search either out of undergraduate or graduate school. It's a lot more difficult to be moving into the industry if you're not currently in it.

Once you're in the industry, however, you'll notice that sales and trading professionals often depart one firm only to immediately set up shop at another firm. This traveling act, so to speak, is very common on the street. It's amazing how many times even a mediocre salesperson can switch firms in a five-year period. Often, these movements are orchestrated by headhunters who get the first three numbers of a firm's telephone number and make random calls to see if there's anyone on the other side of the phone that's willing to make a move. These moves ultimately are determined by the individual, but are seriously influenced by market conditions.

# Licenses and Training

Before you can even talk to a customer or trade a single share of stock, you need to pass the NASD Series 7 and 63 examinations. The Series 7 is the general securities license that every aspiring Wall Streeter needs to have before getting started. It is not an easy exam, so don't blow it off. Failing is embarrassing and a solid study schedule will ensure that you're spared the scorn of your entering class, and more importantly, the disapproval of your potential hiring department.

The Series 63 exam, by comparison is a lot easier. It's basically the exam that every registered representative needs to pass in order to sell securities in other states. Typically, people refer to passing the Series 63 as being "Blue Skied." This means that you can sell securities in any state under the big blue sky.

Recently, the NASDAQ changed its regulations to require that professionals who work on its exchange take the Series 55 exam. This was a result of the $1 billion odd-eighths settlement case in the mid-1990s. It's really a sort of continuing education requirement to make sure the NASDAQ professionals know their execution responsibilities under a constantly changing technology platform. It also tests ethics and professional conduct.

Because you're basically a cost center for your firm until you pass this exam, everything you do for the first few months in an analyst/associate training program is geared towards passing this exam. You will typically come to work, sit in a big classroom with other members of your class and have people talk to you about accounting and bond math. There may even be exams. In between these classroom sessions, you can expect to hear presentations from just about every single major sales and trading department at the firm. This is probably the only time you'll ever get to have such a broad exposure to so many different departments and managing directors, so if you don't pay attention for the bond math or accounting, at least take note of the names of the MDs, VPs and associates who are making the presentations. If you were hired into a generalist pool, the same hustle that got you in the door is going to be absolutely essential for you to get placed in the department that you desire.

Once you've gone through the departmental presentations and the basic bond math and accounting boot camp, you can expect to be placed in a Series 7 training session. The best way to think of this is to think back on your experience taking the Kaplan or Princeton Review classes for the SAT/GMAT. These classes are taught by Series 7 ringers, and they tend to spend a proportional part of their time covering proportionately important parts of the examination. Some of the material on the exam you can actually reason through without memorizing information (e.g., option payoff diagrams), but unfortunately most of it is very fact- and regulation-oriented. Knowing the implications of the Securities Act of 1933 and the Securities Exchange Act of 1934 are more important for the Series 7 than figuring payoff diagrams for various options strategies. And unfortunately, it's not enough just to know that the 1933 Exchange Act deals with offering reporting requirements whereas the 1934 Securities Exchange Act addresses the continuous reporting requirements of corporate issuers. You need to know the differences between Rule 503 and Rule 504 small offering exemptions. You need to know what Regulation A and Regulation D are, and so on, and so on. In short, pay attention in this class and do the assigned readings before your exam.

The Series 7 is a very long exam. It consists of 250 questions and you need to get 70 percent of the questions correct. While it may be your goal is to learn everything inside out to become a knowledgeable securities industry professionally there is no difference between getting a 99 percent and getting a 71 percent on the exam. There is no ranking of analysts/associates based on high grade achievements on an industry exam. After having attended the classes and reviewed the material, it's important to go through the practice exams. The priorities of the NASD are constantly changing, so if you're 24 hours before the exam and have a limited amount of time to study, start with the most current exams, and work backwards if you have time.

The exam is a computer-based exam and is administered by Sylvan Learning Centers, the same friendly folks that you've seen at your other licensing/scholastic standardized tests.

## The Back Office: Backdoor to the Front Office

*The Secret of My Success* chronicles Michael J. Fox's ascent from mail clerk to top corporate gun. A similar story goes on every day on Wall Street's trading desks. The back office is staffed with an army of employees who are responsible for clearing the mountain of trades generated by the front office. The front office speaks with customers to execute trades and revenues. The back office doesn't generate revenues, but its role is vital. If trades are not picked up (DK'ed) or if trade details are different from what the customer knows, this can cost the firm millions of dollars, so it's important to have a back office to keep the business running smoothly. By the very nature of their work (interacting with salespeople and traders on a daily basis to solve problems before they become errors), back office employees have an opportunity to showcase their abilities to the boss. When there's a sales or trading assistant opening in the front office, it often makes sense to fill this position from the back office, since this person is familiar with the trading system, the people and the customers. If you can't immediately get a job in the front office and are desperate to get into trading, consider putting in your dues in the back office for a shot at that dream job. If you do go this route, make sure you have some evidence that the desk you're interested in has a history of hiring from the back office. It's not enough to know that a particular firm may or may not hire from the back office – you need to make inquiries into the specific desk that you're interested in.

# Interview Questions

## CHAPTER 11

The key to nailing your interviews is preparation – and beginning your preparation as soon as possible  It's a lot easier to begin learning finance concepts early and gradually than it is to become a fixed income derivatives expert in two weeks.  We strongly suggest that you begin reading *The Wall Street Journal* and business periodicals such as the *Economist* or *BusinessWeek*.  Sales and trading interviewers, while not overly technical, tend to want to talk about the stock market.  A typical question that you may be asked is, "What do you think about the stock market."  This is a very open-ended question, but the more you are able to tie your market view with current events, the better.

Beyond the news, it's also helpful to try and keep up with the latest market buzz.  You can visit Morgan Stanley's web site to hear the latest from the firm's internal dueling investment strategists, Barton Biggs and Byron Wien.  Another great resource is Bill Gross's market commentary, which is available on PIMCO's web site and is particularly useful for those interested in applying for fixed income positions.  Finally, regardless of the product area you are targeting, it's very useful to know how the economy will impact the markets.  For this, we recommend Professor Jeremy Siegel of the Wharton School.  His class is perennially over-subscribed, and his market commentary is available for free on his web site, JeremySiegel.com.

## Fit Questions

Fit questions are normally the first screen to moving on to the next round of interviews.  These questions are pretty typical investment banking fare, but you should be prepared to talk about why you want to trade or sell.  Make your answer as concrete as possible by offering examples in your past that cause you to believe that you will make a great trader or salesperson.

### 1) Why do you want to become a trader/salesperson?
This question is not so relevant for someone with industry experience, but especially important for career switchers.  Consultants that go back to school to get an MBA to become traders need to have a reason for the career switch.  This story should involve personal reflection and things that you've done in the past that suggest that you might be good at trading in the future.  Maybe

you've traded a personal account and not lost everything. Maybe you're quick with the numbers. For salespeople, the important thing is that you love to sell. If you have a story of a time when you sold ice to Eskimos, by all means, tell it.

### 2) What are your greatest strengths?

Here you want to talk about how you're really quick with numbers, you're analytical, you're motivated and driven and greedy. These strengths need to somehow be related to the job, and if you have personal anecdotes to bolster your claim that you will be God's gift to the currency trading pit, be sure to relay these experiences during your interview.

### 3) What are your greatest weaknesses?

As with any type of interview, you want to make sure that you're not giving away your candidacy by listing serious weaknesses. For example, if your weakness list starts looking like "I'm a poor decision maker under stressful conditions," "I'm not so quick with the numbers" or "I prefer a quiet work environment," perhaps you should consider an alternative to sales and trading.

### 4) What motivates you?

Be sure to mention that in your mind, greed is good (said in a more delicate way of course). Some people talk about wanting to learn from the experience – they are not surprisingly not invited for second-round interviews. Learning is great, but you're paid to earn money. Traders want people that can make money.

If you're a business school student, it may be assumed that you're already too smart for a trading desk, so beware of making yourself look too much like an academic. An acceptable compromise is that you look forward to the steep learning curve (this implies that you'll learn fast) and the opportunity to excel in a true meritocracy. It is debatable whether S&T is actually a true meritocracy, but everyone within the industry tends to view the profession as such.

### 5) How smart are you?

Tricky question. You want to balance off being smart with being someone that people will want to work with. If you end up coming across as a brain attached to a body, then chances are good that you're not going to get a callback. Being smart is a good thing. Being too smart is not.

## 6) What skills have you acquired that will make you appropriate for the job?

This is a really important question for career switchers. A lot of consultants enjoy using a functional resume (a resume organized around skills rather than work history). If you are one of these consultants, then pick the achievements that you feel are most relevant to sales and trading. If you haven't given much thought to this question, think about situations where you have been called on to make decisions under uncertainty, situations that have required a lot of teamwork or a decision that you made that had a material impact on the bottom line.

## 7) How important is money to you?

Remember: greed is good.

## 8) Tell me a good joke.

This is an elaboration on the airport test, which is basically a personality test that asks the interviewer to imagine being stuck at an airport for six hours next to the candidate and to assess whether he or she would be able to tolerate the layover. Make sure you have some jokes handy for your interviews, and with this question, you need to do your best to tailor the joke to your audience.

## 9) Why are you interested in sales and trading rather than investment banking?

This question deserves some thought. You can't really say customer focus, since investment banking and trading are both highly customer-driven activities. You need to think carefully about what in your personality and past work experience makes you more suited to sales and trading versus investment banking. There is some disdain among traders for investment bankers and vice versa, although you'll never get either to admit it. You could potentially use this information to your advantage during the interview, but be careful, since there are always exceptions to the rule.

## 10) How will you motivate yourself to make the calls you hate to make every day?

No one likes making cold calls, but enthusiasm and drive are probably the way to go on this one.

## 11) What is the greatest risk you have ever taken? How risky are you?

There is a common misperception that traders enjoy taking wild amounts of risk. This is simply not true. Traders are paid to take appropriate risks. Be sure that your example demonstrates that you performed due diligence that convinced you that the risk was worth taking, regardless of the eventual outcome.

### 12) What would you add to our firm?

Know the firm you're interviewing with. Know the firm's relative strengths and weaknesses and how you can contribute to the firm's sales and trading capabilities.

### 13) What other firms are you interviewing with?

This is a tough question. You need to consider how much information you're giving out. For example, if you're interviewing with a firm on the edge of the bulge bracket, do you really want to mention that you're interviewing with seven other firms (and are therefore less likely to accept an offer with the firm)? On the other hand, if you say that you're not interviewing with anyone except that firm, you run the risk of sounding desperate or undesirable. You certainly don't want to lie on this one, but be sure to strike the right balance between being highly interested in the firm and being desperate.

Certain firms like to be compared to each other and not to others. While it's common knowledge that Goldman Sachs and Morgan Stanley compete toe-to-toe in just about every business, there are less apparent rivalries that you should be trying to discern throughout the recruiting process. If you know the product area you're interested in, the obvious place to start is the market share/league table. You generally want to make comparisons that the professionals that you're going to be interviewed by are likely making on a daily basis. This is one of the points of differentiation between an unfocused candidate, and one that has done his homework and has sales and trading tattooed all over.

## Market Questions

Traders and salespeople live and breathe the market. You've got to be enthusiastic about your work to be a fierce competitor on the job, and interviewers will try and gauge how much you know about the market, not so much for any particular insight that you may have, but as an indication of your interest for the market.

## 1) Talk to me about the economy.

This question can come in a variety of forms: "Where do you see the dollar trading and how will this impact the long term government bond market?" or "What is your outlook on inflation and do you think there is a risk of deflation?" or "Why is the Federal Reserve so concerned about inflation?" If you are a paying subscriber to *The Wall Street Journal* and wake up to CNBC every morning, you should have no problem with these questions.

## 2) What would you do with $1 million?

A more applied version of this general stock market question is, "Assuming I gave you $1 million to invest, how would you go about investing it?" Here, the obvious point is to talk about products that your interviewer cares about. Don't recommend high yield bonds to an equity salesperson, and don't try and pitch a portfolio of foreign equities to a bond trader. A lot of times, your model portfolio will apparently draw the derision of your interviewer. This is typically going to be a test of your nerves – don't back down. Try to justify your initial portfolio recommendation succinctly and articulately. On the other hand, don't be disagreeable – this is a guaranteed ticket to rejection.

## 3) Tell me about a stock in your personal portfolio.

Salespeople are looking for your ability to pitch the stock, so practice pitching a few stocks in your portfolio. If you're focused on trading, then focus more on the profitability of your trade, and the factors that drive your investing/trading decisions. If you don't own stocks, then you should talk about potential opportunities that exist in the current market environment. While traders are interested in hearing whether or not you are able to make a sound investment decision, remember not to confuse trading with long-term investing – if you have an example where you were speculating based on a short-term market condition, this might be more appropriate than a buy-and-hold investment that you once made.

## 4) Pitch me a stock that you would buy or sell now.

Whatever you do, keep your answer brief. Salespeople and traders have very limited attention spans, so if you find yourself describing what the company does for more than one minute, you're probably not going to sound very convincing. You need to show that you can take the best parts of a stock story and articulate a convincing case quickly. This is what salespeople do every morning, and if you can't do it in in a room with a friendly interviewer, what makes you think you can do it with customers who get calls from 20 salepeople every morning? The ideal scenario here is that you give your pitch, the interviewer asks a few follow-up questions which you are able to discuss intelligently because you are very familiar with the story.

**5) Tell me about three stocks you would buy.**
This question tests your depth of knowledge about the stock market.

# Product Questions

If you say that you love the bond market, then be prepared to answer bond questions. While this is particularly true in fixed income, the same goes for any other product area.

**1) What particular product are you interested in?**
Obviously talk about the bond market if you're going for fixed income. The more successful candidate has done his homework and researched the firm's relative strengths and weaknesses. Generally if you're applying for bonds and find yourself at Lehman or Bear Stearns, this is a pretty easy sell – you'd say that they are the best fixed income franchises on the Street and you've always seen yourself with the best. It's a little more difficult to answer this question if you end up interviewing for a firm that has not yet broken into the top tier of a particular product area. European banks, for example, seem to be perpetually building out their capabilities. However, do not fear – don't be bashful about using the "I'd love to get in on the ground floor and what a great opportunity this is to be selling credit default swaps to the European client base of [name your European bank]."

**2) Why are credit default swaps so popular?**
This type of question can come in a variety of different flavors, but it's a simple screen for how much you care about the business, and how closely you follow the market. If you claim to be a credit default swap enthusiast and can't even explain what they are, Houston, you have a problem. Know the product, know the reasons with the product area is growing and definitely know how the firm you're interviewing fits into the whole picture.

# Valuation and Technical Questions

A further elaboration of the product question is the technical question. If you're a candidate that is targeting a specific product area, then you will likely be asked basic valuation questions. The following questions are common to stocks, bonds and options, but there are a multitude of product areas. Be familiar with how to value the particular product you're interested in.

**1) What are the key points of difference and similarity between a stock and a bond?**

A bond has a fixed maturity and normally pays a specified rate of interest. A stock, on the other hand, represents an ownership share in the firm's assets and profits after senior claimholders (i.e., the bond holders and preferred stock holders) have been satisfied. If there is a dividend, this dividend is variable. Most stocks have voting rights, whereas bond holders typically do not have the right to vote. Both bonds and stocks are negotiable securities.

**2) What's the difference between a primary market and a secondary market?**

The primary market refers to the issuance of new securities. Subsequent to this initial offering, stocks and bonds trade in the secondary market.

**3) What's the difference between a repo and a reverse repo transaction?**

A repo (repurchase agreement) is an agreement for the sale of a security with the simultaneous agreement by the seller to repurchase the security at an agreed upon future date and agreed price. A reverse repo (reverse repurchase agreement) is an agreement for the purchase of a security with the simultaneous agreement by the seller to resell the security at an agreed future date and agreed price. If this sounds like securities lending, that's because it is. Another name for the repo market is the "securities lending market."

**4) The Japanese company NCR issues bonds denominated in British pounds which can only trade in the United Kingdom. What kind of a bond issue is this?**

A foreign bond issue.

**5) What happens to bond prices when yields increase?**

Remember that there is an inverse relationship between bond prices and bond yields. If the yield decreases, then prices increase, and if prices increase then yields decrease. A more confusing version of this question is, "What happens to yields when the price of bonds rallies?" The answer is exactly the same, but it's somewhat tempting to say that yields increase because prices are rallying. Don't fall for this trick.

**6) Why might two bonds issued by the same issuer with the same coupon and the same maturity be trading at a different price?**

A great answer here is to talk about embedded options. You might notice that one bond has an embedded call option, while the other bond does not. Of course, since you the investor are giving up potential upside in the callable bond if interest rates plummet, you're less willing to pay up for the callable bond. Alternatively, you might be willing to pay more for a putable bond, since the issuer has sold you a bond and has thrown in an option that you can use to return the bonds to the issuer if interest rates soar.

**7) I have two bullet bonds of similar maturity and coupon. One trades above the yield curve, the other trades under the yield curve. Which one is the better buy?**

This question tests your knowledge of the inverse price/yield relationship. Remember that a high yield means a cheap dollar price and a low yield means a high dollar price. This means that the better buy is the bond trading over the yield curve.

**8) Is there an exchange of principal in a foreign currency swap?**

You might be tempted to say no, since interest rate swaps do not exchange the notional amounts. However, because a foreign currency swap involves two different currencies, an exchange of principal at the outset and maturity of the swap is necessitated. Also, since there is no common currency upon which interest payments can be netted against, interest payments are paid in full in the two currencies involved in the swap.

**9) Ignoring credit risk, what causes swap spreads to narrow or widen?**

The answer is interest rate expectations. When interest rates are expected to rise, more borrowers want to swap into fixed and receive floating, so swap spreads widen. When interest rates are expected to decline, more borrowers want to swap into floating and receive fixed, causing swap spreads to narrow.

**10) What is put-call parity?**

Put-call parity relates the price of European puts and calls. The put-call parity relationship is expressed by the formula:

$$P = C - S + PV(K)$$

**Where:**

C is the price of the call with the strike price K,

S is the price of the underlying security

P is the price of the put with strike price K.

### 11) What are the limits of duration?

Duration is a useful tool for measuring price volatility, but there are several limitations to its use which are definitely worth knowing.

- Estimates are only valid for small changes in yield. The bigger the assumed change in yield, the more the price/yield convex curvature occurs and the less accurate the estimate.

- Duration assumes a parallel yield-curve shift, even though yield curves very rarely shift in a uniform fashion.

- Duration does not account for yield volatility.

- Duration cannot value bonds with embedded options. Duration implicitly assumes that cash flows are completely known and unchangeable. In the real world, bonds are callable and putable.

### 12) Assume a Treasury bond and a junk bond are issued at the same time and with the same maturity. Which bond has a greater duration?

The answer is the Treasury bond. If you went for the junk bond answer, then you have an incomplete understanding of duration which needs to be remedied. Duration is higher because the Treasury bond carries a lower coupon rate, which raises duration relative to the higher coupon junk bond. Does this mean that the Treasury bond has greater price volatility? To answer this question, you need to consider yield volatility. The price volatility of the bond is a combination of duration and yield volatility.

### 13) Why do yield curves invert?

Typically the cost of borrowing increases as maturity increases. An inverted yield curve is an uncommon situation in which long-term interest rates are lower than short-term interest rates. Yield curves tend to invert following periods of tight money and tight credit, and when the curve inverts, the market is expecting that short-term interest rates will decline.

**14) Assume an inverted yield curve. How do I make money in bonds if I expect the yield curve to revert?**

If the yield curve reverts to its normal shape (upward sloping), then short-term rates must rise more than long-term rates. This means that you want to put on a curve-steepening trade where you are buy long-term maturities and are short short-term maturities. This is a generic trade in the government bond market, and the spreads between two years and 30 years, two years and 10 years, two years and five years, and so on, are constantly quoted, especially ahead of Fed action and the release of widely anticipated economic statistics.

Be sure to know how to make money if the yield curve flattens.

**15) What's the difference between a stock exchange and a futures exchange?**

Remember that a share of stock represents a fractional ownership interest in a company, whereas a futures contract represents the obligation to accept or deliver a quantity of a commodity on a pre-specified future date. The difference between these two exchanges is how a price is determined. On the NYSE (remember NASDAQ is not an exchange), the specialist maintains an orderly market, whereas on the futures exchange, price is discovered through an open outcry market.

**16) What is the duration of a zero coupon bond?**

Duration is a measure of the interest rate sensitivity of the payments of a bond. Zero coupon bonds differ from conventional bonds in that there are no interest payments. Zero coupon bonds are issued at a discount and investors receive a single par payment at maturity. Since the amount and timing of this cash flow occurs independent of interest rates, the duration of a zero coupon bond is simply equal to its maturity. So a 30-year zero coupon bond has a maturity of 30 years and a duration of 30 years. The duration of a 30-year conventional bond is substantially less than 30 years.

**17) What is the delta of an at-the-money option?**

Delta measures the change in the option value for a unit change in the underlying security. An at-the-money option refers to an option whose strike price currently equals the price of the underlying security. For example, an IBM June 80 call is at the money if IBM stock is trading at exactly $80 per share. At this price, there is a 50% chance that the stock will move "in the money" (over $80 per share) and there is a 50 percent chance that the stock will move "out of the money" (under $80 per share), so the delta of the at-the-money option is 0.50.

# Brainteasers

Brainteasers are especially common at the undergraduate level, where recruiters have little else than a GPA and school pedigree to separate one candidate for another. For equity-related positions, it used to be very common for people to ask interviewers to calculate 7/16ths or 14/32nds to three decimals. The reasoning here is that a lot of what happens on the desk is fast paced, and if you buy something at 7/16ths and then strike a deal to sell it at 13/32nds, you're out 3 cents on whatever volume you're transacting. Now that the stock market has decimalized, this question is a lot less prevalent, but you can still expect to be quizzed on your 32nds from the fixed income side. One word of warning: if you're not comfortable doing quick arithmetic on your feet, you're probably not going to last long on a sales and trading desk.

**1) What is the expected value of a roll of a dice?**
Most traders, particularly the options traders, are very fond of asking questions about dice and playing cards. Pay attention in your statistics class – chances are very good that you'll have someone ask you a basic probability question. By the way, the answer to the question is $3\frac{1}{2}$, not 3.

**2) Make me a price on the 8 serial numbers on a $1 bill.**
This is a test of your familiarity with expected value. Expected value refers to what you can expect, on average. In this example, you have nine possible choices for any one digit. The expected value of any one digit is 5 (1,2,3 and 4 are below 5 and 6,7,8,9 are above 5). Therefore for an eight-digit serial number, the expected value is: 55555555.

**3) What is the probability of flipping 3 heads and 1 tail?**
This is a gambler's trap. Coin flips are memory-less and there's just as much a chance of rolling four heads as there are rolling of rolling two heads and two tails or three heads and one tail, etc. Each outcome has a probability of $(0.5)^4 = .0625$. Don't get trapped thinking that there's more of a chance that the fourth flip will be a tail just because the previous three flips were heads.

# Decrease your T/NJ Ratio
## (Time to New Job)

Use the Internet's most targeted job search tools for finance professionals.

## Vault Finance Job Board

The most comprehensive and convenient job board for finance professionals. Target your search by area of finance, function, and experience level, and find the job openings that you want. No surfing required.

## VaultMatch Resume Database

Vault takes match-making to the next level: post your resume and customize your search by area of finance, experience and more. We'll match job listings with your interests and criteria and e-mail them directly to your inbox.

VΛULT
> the most trusted name in career information™

# Exit Options

## CHAPTER 12

Most people who get into sales or trading don't really fully understand what they're really getting into. Many hope to have made enough money by age 30 to retire. Unfortunately, the reality is that very few people are good traders, and selling to the Fidelities and Capital Groups of the world is becoming an increasingly difficult business to break into, especially in a business where relationships mean everything.

Having said that, sales and trading can be an incredibly rewarding career for the right person. Several practical suggestions – consider joining a firm that has the flexibility to move you around if you're willing to move. Of course, this isn't going to be an option when you blow up one of the firm's major accounts and then ask to be transferred to PCS. Instead, this exit option is premised on your doing a good job and being profitable, and then maybe asking for the possibility of moving over to the capital markets side of the business because you want to pursue an interest in larger transactions and closer customer interaction. Several firms are very good at this; others are not. As mentioned previously, Goldman Sachs has a tremendous reputation for encouraging movement of its personnel between offices and divisions.

In the following sections, we take a look at some of the common options if you want to leave sales and trading at a sell-side firm.

## Business School

The primary exit option for analysts is to go back to business school. This option is not as automatic is it is within the investment banking analyst classes. Typically, under normal market conditions, trading desks will invite successful analysts to stay on as an associate. This is a strong vote of confidence, and most analysts will end up choosing to stay on. However, if it at this stage in your career you realize that you're good at what you do but you want to do something else, this might be a good time to have a conversation with your manager to consider relocating or perhaps trying another more interesting product area. Alternatively, if you decide that you've had enough of the business, then the best thing to do is apply to business school. Of course, if your career is less than successful, you will already have requested applications for business school.

The main difference between undergraduate analysts and MBA associates is that MBAs have a quicker path to promotion and sales/trading responsibility. MBAs fetch coffee for weeks rather than months, and can expect to start trading fairly soon. If this is not happening, then there is something probably wrong with the firm or with the MBA. The scary thing for MBAs is that once they're on the trading desk, they better be sure that this is what they want to do for the long run. The sales and trading profession offers far fewer legitimate career exits than other MBA career tracks like consulting. Most exit options in this business relate to switching firms rather than industries. It is very likely that in a good market you'll be able to switch firms, but if you're deeply dissatisfied with sales or trading, this change of scenery is probably going to get old very quickly.

# Debt or Equity Capital Markets

Capital markets professionals work with the investment banking and sales and trading departments to sell debt or equity offerings. Capital markets professionals sit on the trading desk, and therefore work better hours than investment bankers, but somewhat longer hours than the traders who breeze out of the office at 4:01 p.m. A capital markets professional can be called upon to perform comparable analysis, to help structure a deal, to participate in client meetings and road shows and to advise investment bankers about the price of a debt or equity offering. This sounds an awful lot like the job description of an investment banker. The primary difference is that capital market professionals have more of a market focus, whereas investment bankers are more focused on a product group. It is this market and client focus that makes a successful trader or sales professional eligible for consideration in this capacity.

# The Buy-Side

Sell-side traders often pine for the buy-side, where the hours are equally nice and the work is a lot less stressful. Buy-side traders act as intermediaries between Wall Street sharks and spectacled portfolio managers. While the buy-side trader does not have to provide liquidity, he is responsible for executing orders on a best efforts basis. Best efforts means that the buy-side trader is getting the best possible price for each and every order – essentially, his primary responsibility is to keep the sell-side trader honest. The bigger the buy-side shop, the bigger the trading staff and the more difficult it is for the sell-side to make an "honest buck."

Buy-side trading is very different from sell-side trading. The buy-side trader acts as the go-between between the portfolio manager and the sales-trader/salesperson. The buy-side trader is also responsible for passing along timely market information to the portfolio manager customers that he or she represents in the marketplace. To get the job done, the effective buy-side trader must have extensive relationships with executing brokers. He must also have the trust of his client, the portfolio manager. The best way to think of it is to put yourself in their position. As a sell-side trader you're always trying to nickel-and-dime the buy-side. The buy-sider (often an ex-sell-sider) knows this and is always vigilant for the unscrupulous sell-side.

Imagine a portfolio manager that has been trying to sell an illiquid trucking stock for two weeks and all of a sudden large bids start popping up out of nowhere. The proactive buy-side trader has a conversation with the PM, and passes along this valuable market information – rather than hit the bids immediately, maybe there's an opportunity to sell this illiquid trucker at a higher price. The buy-side trader could figure out who is showing the bids, determine the buyer's appetite and place the shares with another institutional account. This buyer is a "natural buyer," and it's the most desirable transaction from the seller's perspective, since it is orderly and it minimizes slippage costs.

# Hedge Funds

Another attractive venue for successful traders and salespeople is the hedge fund community. Hedge funds operate large pools of capital, but are substantially less regulated than the mutual fund industry. Hedge funds offer specialized investment expertise and are committed to one particular strategy (e.g., convertible arbitrage, risk arbitrage, market-neutral long/short equity, and so on). (See the sidebar on hedge fund strategies on the next page.) Larger hedge funds can allocate pools of capital to several strategies – these hedge funds are called multi-strategy funds. Although there are a myriad of fund strategies that can be pursued, the most common type of hedge fund is the long/short equity hedge fund.

Good traders can thrive in the hedge fund environment. Hedge funds tend to emphasize speculative short-term profits, and traders with an ability to generate a consistent profit are in high demand. Salespeople are also in high demand if they have a developed book of business and contacts that can eventually lead to substantial investments in the hedge fund. Salespeople at hedge funds are expected to prospect for new contacts, sell new subscription interests and review portfolio performance with existing customers. Their importance, especially in a start-up hedge fund environment cannot be overstated.

The downside to hedge funds is that they're inherently less stable organizations, even relative to high-turnover investment banks. Salespeople and traders at hedge funds accept a great deal of career risk, since their compensation is substantially tied to their commission runs and trading revenues. Hedge fund careers have the volatility of the markets and their organizational structures are always in flux. Funds are always being created, unwound, merged or separated, and these changes can produce unexpected windfall gains or losses from a career perspective.

# Hedge Fund Strategies

## Long/short equity strategy

The long/short equity strategy is the most prevalent hedge fund strategy. Rather than just taking leveraged directional bets on the stock market, long/short funds buy and sell stocks based on the belief that one firm's stock will outperform another firm's stock. By buying the star and shorting the dog, long/short equity funds hedge away the market risk in the position. Portfolio performance is driven entirely by the hedge fund manager's ability to pick stocks. Certain hedge funds are more short-term trading-oriented than others. The best way to break into this industry is to work with a headhunter that specializes in the hedge fund industry.

## Other hedge fund strategies

Macro hedge funds take positions on macroeconomic events throughout the world. Perhaps the most infamous retired hedge fund operator is George Soros, who gained notoriety when his Quantum hedge fund bet big against the British pound and netted a profit exceeding $1 billion.

Global hedge funds take positions in regions throughout the world, including emerging markets. Long Term Capital Management's exposure to illiquid Russian bonds led to its demise, and triggered a short-lived financial crisis. Other hedge funds specialize on long-only, short-only or sector-specific strategies. Event driven hedge funds seek to capitalize on perceived market mispricings related to bankruptcies or mergers.

## Funds-of-funds

Finally, there is the fund-of-funds organization, which is responsible for allocating capital across a portfolio of hedge fund investments. Funds-of-funds scrutinize individual managers in the same way that a traditional portfolio manager analyzes stocks for potential investment. Funds-of-funds are concerned with the long-term performance record of the investment manager, and the style-discipline of the manager who has received a mandate. For example, a fund-of-funds firm that gave a 5 percent allocation to a convertible arbitrage fund will want to insure that over time, the hedge fund manager is in fact faithfully investing in convertible arbitrage situations and not straying away from the strategy that he was hired to implement.

# Day Trading

This option has lost a lot of its appeal since the technology stock bubble burst in March of 2000. Nevertheless, traders who decide to call it quits with the customer-oriented flow trading business are often attracted to day trading. Day traders attempt to capture very short-term profits, and they exploit the best direct-access trading technology available at a number of different day trading firms. These firms offer a comprehensive trading platform, and most also offer risk capital in exchange for an agreement to trade using the firm's software package and the related commission dollar stream that you are expected to generate. Before you try your hand at day trading, be aware of several things. First, this risk capital is not free. Firms will normally take their cut out of your profits and they will also require you to cover your losses in full. What this means is that if you make money, you're only making a fraction of what you generate, but if you lose money, you're entirely responsible for the loss. Several firms have less stringent rules around your trading losses, but before you sign on, be sure you know the rules of the game, and as with any type of trading, be sure that you're able to handle the significant downside written into this arrangement.

The latest iteration at day trading firms is to offer commission rebates to day traders that are adding liquidity to the marketplace. If your order is adding liquidity to the marketplace (i.e., your order enhances the depth of the market), the you will be entitled to a rebate on the order if it is executed. On the other hand, if your order is taking liquidity out of the market, (i.e., your order is reducing the depth of the market), then you will be charged a higher commission rate.

# APPENDIX

Recommended Reading

Glossary and Industry Jargon

About the Author

# Recommended Reading

The best thing to do is to immerse yourself in the markets. Say goodbye to the *Today* show and hello to CNBC. Read *The Wall Street Journal*, and if you're really enterprising, you'll take out a subscription to *Investor's Business Daily*. Although you can't sit on a trading desk, there is a ton of literature available for you to read. Several books that are worth mentioning are:

Stocks for the Long Run by Jeremy Siegel gives a great overview of the stock market, and is a must if you're interested in equity sales and trading.

Similarly, Frank Fabozzi's guide book, Handbook of Fixed Income Securities is an essential component for any budding bond trader's bookshelf. It's not particularly easy to read, but you can pick and choose your spots.

A great book to read about technical analysis is William O'Neil's How to Make Money in Stocks, which features the cup and handle chart pattern. Another classic is Sam Weinstein's Secrets for Profiting in Bull and Bear Markets.

Hull's Options, Futures and Other Derivatives gives a good overview of derivative products. Among other things, it describes option pricing methodologies and options and futures payoff diagrams.

To help decipher your economics textbook, you should read By the Numbers: A Survival Guide to Economic Indicators by Slifer and Carnes. This book is written from the perspective of a consumer of economic statistics, and spends a lot of time explaining what's important in economic data from the market's perspective.

Several other books that are recommended for entertainment purposes include Liar's Poker by Michael Lewis, which gives you an insider's perspective on the culture of greed at Salomon Brothers. Reminiscences of a Stock Operator by Edwin Lefevre and The Market Wizards series by Jack Schwager provides first hand accounts and interviews with some of the best traders of our time. Since institutional traders are frequently taking the other side of a speculator's trade, each book provides a valuable perspective on how successful people in the business think and approach the markets.

# Glossary and Industry Jargon

## Equity Glossary

Learning the language of the business is half the battle. What follows is a brief review of some of the most heavily used terms that you'll hear on an equity sales and trading desk.

**Agency trading:** NASDAQ agency traders execute orders in stocks that the firm does not maintain a market in "on an agency basis." Customer trades executed by the firm's position traders are executed on a principal basis.

**Black-Scholes option pricing model:** Before Fischer Black and Myron Scholes blew themselves up at Long Term Capital Management, they sat atop the pinnacle of modern finance theory, rubbing elbows with Miller and Modigliani. Black-Scholes is an options pricing model that prices options according to the current stock price, the time until option expiration, the option strike price, the risk-free interest rate, the standard deviation of stock returns, and the cumulative standard normal distribution.

*The Black-Scholes model makes several key assumptions:*

- The stock pays no dividends during the life of the option
- European exercise terms (option exercise at expiry only) are used
- Efficient markets
- No commissions
- Constant and known interest rates
- Returns are lognormally distributed.

**Convertible bond:** A convertible bond can be exchanged for a pre-specified amount of common stock in the issuing firm. The conversion ratio indicates the number of shares of common stock that the holder of the convertible has a claim. The conversion price is derived by dividing the par value divided by the conversion ratio.

**Delta hedging:** A strategy designed to reduce the risk associated with price movements in the underlying security, achieved through offsetting long and short positions of calls and puts. Delta-hedging strategies can be either dynamic or static. A dynamic-hedging strategy involves the portfolio being rebalanced periodically to maintain a targeted delta. A hedging strategy that is never rebalanced after the initial hedge is initiated is called static-hedging.

**ECN:** ECNs, or Electronic Crossing Networks are direct-access trading systems that bypass broker-dealers. Investors and traders are able to input their orders and have them displayed directly on the NASDAQ or the NYSE. Typically, ECNs charge a much lower per share commission than a full-service broker dealer.

**Exchange-traded funds (ETFs):** ETFs are a basket of securities designed to track an index and trade like a single stock. Currently there are more than 100 exchange-traded ETFs, and the largest and most liquid ETFs are Spiders (SPY) which track the S&P500, Diamonds (DIA) which track the Dow Jones Industrial Average and the QQQs, which track the NASDAQ 100.

**Ex-dividend date:** The day a stock trades without the dividend. Technically, on the ex-dividend date, the price of the stock should adjust downward by the amount of the dividend that will be paid out on the payment date.

**Indication:** An indication is an estimated price, not a firm quote. When the NYSE has a buy or sell order imbalance, it publishes an indication, which is an estimated range for the stock's opening price. This indication often attracts buy or sell interest, and the indication is updated to reflect this new interest, and eventually the stock is opened. On the NASDAQ, every pre-opening quote is deemed to be an indication.

Throughout the trading day, traders may be asked for a quote on a bond or a stock. The typical quoting convention is that these prices are "indications only," and that before a salesperson is able to transact, he must double-check with the trader to get a "firm quote" which is a price and quantity that the trader will honor.

**Momentum trading:** Momentum traders seek to exploit the very short-term momentum in the market. In its simplest form, momentum traders believe that "the trend is your friend" and will buy stocks that are exploding on the upside and shorting stocks that are breaking down. This type of trading can potentially do well in trending markets, but will tend to do poorly in range-bound markets.

**P/E ratio:** The P/E ratio measures the current price of the security divided by a full year of earnings. Price is pretty obvious, but there are several things you need to consider with earnings. Forward EPS is the expectation for the next 12 months of earnings. LTM, (last 12 months) is trailing earnings. Since most firms are growing their earnings, Forward P/E ratios will normally be lower than trailing P/E ratios.

**Preferred stock:** Preferred stock shares characteristics of both common stock and debt. Preferred stockholders are entitled to dividends as a specified percentage of par. If these dividends can accrue until they are paid, the preferred stock issue is called a cumulative preferred stock. If the dividend payment can be missed, then the preferred stock is called a non-cumulative preferred stock. Dividend payments on preferred stock are not tax deductible to the issuing corporation.

**Program trading:** Program trading is a generic term used to describe a type of trading in securities driven by computer-assisted trading programs. These strategies usually involve the trading of stocks, their corresponding options, and index futures and options. The trading of these securities and indices is based purely on their price in relation to each other on a predetermined basis, and not on company-specific fundamentals. The most common type of program trading is index arbitrage, which exploits the miniscule price differences between indices and their constituent stocks. According to the NYSE, program trading accounts for about 30 percent of average daily trading volume.

**Put/call ratio:** The put/call ratio is the number of put options contracts traded in a given day divided by the number of call options contracts traded that same day. The put volume divided by the call volume yields the put/call ratio. The put/call ratio is used as a contrarian indicator: the greater the number of puts that are traded, the more bearish is the market and the more bullish the informed speculator is supposed to become. On the other hand, the greater the number of calls that are traded, the more bullish the market has become and this should correspond to a more bearish stance for the informed speculator.

**SelectNet:** SelecNet was an automated trading service that allowed broker/dealers to trade with each other electronically. SelectNet allowed market makers to preference each other and was typically used to execute trades between the bid-ask spread. SelectNet was replaced by SuperSOES.

**Short interest:** Short interest refers to how many shares are sold short in a given stock. Short interest is normally interpreted as a contrarian indicator. Large short-interest represents future demand (i.e., at some point these bearish bets need to be covered), and shares that everyone hates and that everyone has sold short can experience volatile moves to the upside (think Amazon). The days-to-cover ratio is the number of shares short divided by the average daily trading volume. The larger this ratio, the more likely the stock is setting up for a short-squeeze.

**Small Order Execution System (SOES):** SOES was implemented by NASDAQ in 1985 as a response to the 1987 market crash. During the Crash, market makers simply refused to pick up the phone to take customer orders. SOES was originally conceived as a small order execution system that automatically executed against a market maker's display size, thereby reducing the possibility that dealers use and abuse the small investor. It didn't take long before a new breed of electronic trader was born: the SOES bandit. SOES bandits used the execution system to scalp profits from dealer spreads. Dealers complained as SOES bandits ate their lunch. The newest version of SOES, SuperSOES is essentially the next generation in NASDAQ order execution. This latest version consolidates SOES and SELECTNET, and is supposed to reduce dual liability and improve trading efficiency.

You can read more about the electronic gamesmanship between SOES bandits and NASDAQ market makers in Electronic Day Trading by David Nassar.

**SuperDOT:** SuperDot ("Designated Order Turnaround") is a computerized system that can send orders of up to 99,999 shares directly to the NYSE specialist's computerized order book. SuperDOT bypasses the floor broker and currently over 90 percent of the NYSE's orders and 45 percent of the shares that trade on the NYSE are executed through SuperDOT. SuperDOT is an electronic order delivery system, not an order execution system. Consequently, SuperDOT orders are visible only at the specialist post, and not off the floor. For this reason, large institutional orders are not sent over SuperDOT – the floor has an instant information advantage over the person who sent the order.

**Technical analysis:** The discipline of studying past price movements to predict future price performance. Traders frequently rely on charts to identify areas of support and resistance, and certain chart formations, such as the double bottom or the head and shoulders top or bottom reversal.

**Triple witching (hour):** An event that occurs four times a year: the 3rd Friday of March, June, September and December. On these days, contracts for stock index futures, stock index options and stock options all expire on the same day. Triple witching produces a great deal of volatility, especially in underlying securities that are at or near at-the-money levels. Investors that are long at-the-money options have a financial interest in pushing the price of the underlying security above the strike price, whereas dealers (who are typically option sellers) have an interest in keeping the price of the underlying security below the strike price.

**VIX (Volatility Index):** The VIX measures implied volatility in S&P 100 options. This implied volatility can be calculated from the option premiums and an options pricing formula. The VIX is employed by traders as a tool for measuring investor fear. High readings (above 50) typically mark periods of maximum fear and have pinpointed important market bottoms. Low readings (below 20), while not as accurate and timely as high readings, illustrate investor complacency and usually are a waning sign pointing towards market tops.

**Warrants:** A warrant is a derivative security that grants the holder the right (but not the obligation) to purchase stock from the issuer at a specific price within a certain period of time. There are two main differences between a warrant and a call. First, warrants are much longer-dated securities. Warrants are also issued and guaranteed by the issuer, whereas call options are exchange-traded securities. Warrants are normally issued in conjunction with a debt offering, to make the deal more attractive to prospective bond buyers. This extra privilege granted to bond investors hurts the common shareholder because it dilutes the existing shareholder's interest in the ownership structure of the firm.

# Fixed Income Glossary

As with the equity business, there's a lot of bond language that needs to be learned. You'll also need to learn the bond math, some of which is provided here but you'll need to find a fixed income reference book, and here again you can't go wrong with Frank Fabozzi's, Handbook of Fixed Income Securities.

**Barbell:** A bond trading strategy with which the trader holds long-term and short-term bonds. In this case, the trader is anticipating a profit based on the view that long and short-term bonds will outperform intermediate-term bonds.

**Bond equivalent yield:** Doubling the semiannual yield.

**Bond rating agencies:** The main bond rating agencies are Standard & Poor's and Moody's. The role of the rating agencies is to provide an unbiased opinion of the issuer's credit-worthiness. Arguably, this analysis is more objective than equity analysis, since the sole criteria that is applied is the ability of the issuer to repay its debts. Other secondary bond rating agencies include Fitch's and Duff & Phelps.

**Bond ratings:** Bonds are classified into two groups – "investment grade" bonds and "junk" bonds. Investment grade bonds include those assigned to the top four quality categories by either Standard & Poor's (AAA, AA, A, BBB) or Moody's (Aaa, Aa, A, Baa). Investment grade bonds are generally legal for purchase by banks; junk bonds are not. Bonds that cross the threshold from investment grade to junk bonds must be purged from most institutional accounts, creating potential profit opportunities for the discerning distressed debt investor.

The term "junk" is reserved for all bonds with Standard & Poor's ratings below BBB and/or Moody's ratings below Baa. Junk bond ratings include BB, B, CCC, CC, C and D. BB-rated bonds have the lowest degree of speculation (among junk bonds) while a D rating is assigned to an issuer in default of payment. As the investor reaches for higher yield by stepping down the credit rating spectrum, he is accepting less quality and protective characteristics (i.e., interest coverage) and assuming greater financial risk.

**Bullet:** A regular coupon paying bond with a single repayment of principal (the bullet) on the maturity date.

**Current yield:** Current yield = Annual dollar coupon interest/Price

**Convexity:** The formula for convexity is rather unwieldy. Remember that the price/yield relationship of a bond is inverse and convex. Duration is a straight-line estimate. Conceptually, convexity is the prediction error between the straight-line duration estimate and the convex price/yield curve. The equation for convexity is:

Convexity (in years) =

$$1*2*PVCF1 + 2*3*PVCF2 +...N* (N+1)*PVCFN/[(1+YTM/2)^2*k^2*PVTCF]$$

Where:

k = the number of periods (payments) per year, so k = 2 for a semiannual pay bond)
N = Number of periods until maturity (Years to maturity*k)
PVCFT = Present value of the cash flow in period t discounted at the YTM
PVTCF = Total present value of the cash flows of the bond where the present value is determined using the bond's YTM.

The approximate percentage price change due to convexity =
0.5*Convexity*(Yield change)^2*100

The approximate percentage price change based on duration and convexity is additive:

Estimated percentage price change =
-Modified duration*Yield change*100 + 0.5*Convexity*(Yield change)^2*100

For option-free bonds, convexity is always positive. Bonds with embedded options that the investor is short (think callable bonds and mortgage-backed securities where the investor is short the prepayment option) exhibit negative convexity. If bond yields fall far enough, negative convexity limits the upside price appreciation relative to an option-free bond. For example, if bond yields fall far enough, then issuers will realize a gain by calling the bond away from the investors at the lower call price. Similarly, mortgage owners will exercise their prepayment option with greater frequency if bond yields fall. In a lower interest rate environment, mortgage holders have an incentive to prepay the higher rate mortgage so that they can refinance at the lower, current rate. This prepayment results in an earlier than expected return of principal to the MBS investor, who must also contend with lower reinvestment rates.

**Duration:** Duration describes of the sensitivity of a bond's price to a change in yield.

**Effective annual yield (EAY):**

EAY = (1+ periodic interest rate)^k – 1
Where k is the number of payments per year

For example, if I have a bond with a 5% semi-annual interest rate, the effective annual yield is:

EAY = (1.05)^2 – 1
EAY = 10.25%

Although this is the mathematically correct way to annualize a semiannual interest rate, most market practitioners use the bond-equivalent yield.

**Effective duration:** Effective duration is a duration measure that quantifies the price sensitivity of the bond while also allowing for changes in the bond's expected cash flows. The methodology for computing effective duration requires the use of a binomial interest-rate tree.

**Eurodollar:** An American dollar held by a foreign institution outside the U.S., usually a bank in Europe.

**LIBOR:** The London Inter-bank Offer Rate is the rate that is the interest rate that the largest international banks charge each other for loans usually denominated in Eurodollars.

**Macaulay duration:** Macaulay duration measures the price volatility of a bond. The concept was first formulated by Frederick Macaulay in 1938. Macualay duration is a weighted average of the bond's cash flows where the weights are the present value of each cash flow as a percentage of the bond's full price.

Macaulay Duration = 1*PVCF1 + 2*PVCF2 + 3*PVCF3...+N*PVCFN/ (k*PVTCF)

Where:

The terms are the same as defined under the convexity equation

If you don't totally understand duration, just remember that the longer the duration of the bond, the greater is its percentage price volatility.

**Marked-to-market:** A trader's profit and loss statement is marked-to-market. This refers to the daily valuation of the trader's account to reflect current market prices. The goal of every trader is to make his P&L statement as large and positive as possible. Some times, traders will make money trading, but will lose money because a large position goes down. The trader's explanation to the boss will go something like this: "I traded pretty well, but this piece of crap position was marked down $100,000."

**Medium term note (MTN):** A medium-term note is a program of bond issues for a specified total amount of bonds over a specified period of time. MTNs are usually unsecured, fixed or floating rate, non-callable debt securities. MTNs save issuers time and money by allowing them to register a program of issuance rather than a series of separate bond issues.

**Modified duration:** Modified duration measures the sensitivity of the bond's price to changes in the yield to maturity. It assumes a flat-term structure of interest rates and that yield changes do not change the bond's cash flow.

Modified duration = Macaulay duration / 1 + (YTM/k)

Modified duration can then be used to estimate the percentage price change:

Percentage price change = -Modified duration*Yield change*100

The operative word here is estimate. Duration estimates are linear and symmetric, but if you've taken an elementary finance course, you know that the price/yield relationship is not linear and not symmetric. Convexity improves duration by estimating the curvature of the price/yield relationship.

**On-the-runs:** On-the-runs issues are those bonds most recently issued in each maturity. Off-the-runs refer to everything else. All else being equal an on-the-run bond will trade at a slightly lower yield than the comparable off-the-run bond. This difference in yield reflects the liquidity premium offered by trading the most current bond.

**Option-adjusted spread (OAS):** A fixed income security's implied risk premium above the risk-less rate. The OAS is the spread above the risk-free rate that makes the average present value of the security's cash flows equal to the market price of the security. The OAS of a risk-free security is zero.

**Option-payoff diagram:** These diagrams indicate the expected profit of an option strategy at expiry. Options allow investors to hedge risk in long and short positions. Combining options can create the desired risk-reward profile for the options trader. Options strategies that are worth knowing are the butterfly spread, condor spread, bull and bear spreads, calendar spread, straddle, strangles and portfolio insurance.

**Prepayment model:** Mortgage holders typically have the right to prepay all or part of their mortgage. Therefore, to properly value mortgage-backed securities, investors must make some sort of assumption of the prepayment rate on the underlying mortgage collateral. Two simple prepayment models are the Constant Prepayment Rate (CPR) and the Public Securities Association (PSA) model. Wall Street is always tinkering with proprietary econometric prepayment models which try to better estimate prepayment rates based on a collection of explanatory variables.

**Price value of a basis point (PVBP):** PVBP is a measure of price volatility for a bond. It measures the change in yield for a one basis point change in price.

**Primary dealer:** A designation awarded by the Federal Reserve to commercial banks or broker/dealers who meet specific criteria, most notably capital requirements and participation in Treasury auctions.

**Redemption classification:** Most bonds are bullets, but sometimes bonds have embedded options that alter the structure of a bond such that the principal may be repaid prior to maturity. A callable bond gives the issuer the right but not the obligation to redeem a bond at strike prices and dates before the bond is scheduled to mature. Putable bonds give the investor the right but not the obligation to put the bond back to the issuer. A sinking fund bond retires a portion of the principal according to an agreed schedule. A sinking fund can be thought of as a series of call options that the investor writes to the issuer, except that a sinking fund provision is obligatory rather than just a right. Perpetual bonds pay a coupon to the investor forever. Call options are often embedded within perpetual bonds to give the issuer an opportunity to return this perpetual obligation.

**Yield curve:** The yield curve graphically represents the relationship between the yield on bonds of the same credit quality but different maturities. The most commonly quoted yield curve is the Treasury yield curve, which is assumed to be free of default risk. Other yield curves are quoted as a spread over the Treasury yield curve.

**Yield-to-maturity (YTM):** The YTM is the interest rate that will make the present value of the cash flows of the bond equal to the price of the bond. The major shortfall of YTM is that this measure assumes that there is no reinvestment risk, i.e. that coupons can be reinvested at a rate that is equal to the YTM. Another way of stating this is that the yield curve is flat. This is rarely ever the case and YTM is almost always never realized.

# About the Author

**Gabriel Kim** studied at the Wharton School of the University of Pennsylvania, first as an undergraduate in the Management and Technology dual degree program and then as an MBA. Gabriel managed an equity hedge fund, and traded equities for ING Barings and Lehman Brothers. Gabriel has been passionate about the stock market ever since his first purchase of Dell Computer shares during high school.

# Decrease your T/NJ Ratio
## (Time to New Job)

Use the Internet's most targeted

job search tools for finance

professionals.

## Vault Finance Job Board

The most comprehensive and convenient job board for finance
professionals. Target your search by area of finance, function,
and experience level, and find the job openings that you want.
No surfing required.

## VaultMatch Resume Database

Vault takes match-making to the next level: post your resume
and customize your search by area of finance, experience and
more. We'll match job listings with your interests and criteria
and e-mail them directly to your inbox.

VAULT
> the most trusted name in career information™

# Decrease your T/NJ Ratio
## (Time to New Job)

Use the Internet's most targeted job search tools for finance professionals.

## Vault Finance Job Board

The most comprehensive and convenient job board for finance professionals. Target your search by area of finance, function, and experience level, and find the job openings that you want. No surfing required.

## VaultMatch Resume Database

Vault takes match-making to the next level: post your resume and customize your search by area of finance, experience and more. We'll match job listings with your interests and criteria and e-mail them directly to your inbox.

VAULT
> the most trusted name in career information™